BERKSHIRE OUTDOORS

Hikes
&Walks

Hikes &Walks

IN THE BERKSHIRE HILLS
Revised Edition

TEXT BY LAUREN R. STEVENS

Illustrations by Alison Kolesar
Maps by Alison Kolesar and Vaughan Gray

Berkshire House Publishers
Lee, Massachusetts

The text of this book was designed and composed by Jane McWhorter. The typefaces are Palatino and Helvetica. Cover photograph © Coco McCoy/Rainbow. Hiking maps by Alison Kolesar are based on U.S. Geological Survey Quadrants. Vaughan Gray drew the supplementary maps. Map on p. 109 is adapted from "Pittsfield: A Self-Guided Historic Walking Tour" by Pittsfield Central.

Library of Congress Cataloging-in-Publication Data
Stevens, Lauren R., 1938-
Hikes & walks in the Berkshire Hills / text by Lauren R. Stevens ; illustrations by Alison Kolesar ; maps by Alison Kolesar and Vaughan Gray.
    p.   cm. — (Berkshire outdoors)
Includes bibliographical references (p.).
ISBN 0-936399-94-5
1. Hiking — Massachusetts — Berkshire Hills — Guidebooks.
2. Walking — Massachusetts — Berkshire Hills — Guidebooks.
3. Berkshire Hills (Mass.) — Guidebooks.
I. Title. II. Series.
GV199.42.M42B47 1998
917.44'10443 — dc21   97-46408   CIP

Editor: Glen Novak

Berkshire House Publishers
480 Pleasant Street
Lee, Massachusetts 01238
800-321-8526
E-mail: info@berkshirehouse.com
Website: www.berkshirehouse.com

Manufactured in the United States of America

10 9 8 7 6 5 4 3 2

BERKSHIRE, THE BERKSHIRES, THE BERKSHIRE HILLS

What is the name of this place, anyway? The original Berkshire is in England, south of Oxford. There it's pronounced "Bark-shuh." "Shire" refers to an Anglo-Saxon administrative district.

Purists refer to the "Berkshire Hills," meaning specifically what this book calls the southern Taconics, including peaks in New York State. The logic of calling all hills in Berkshire County the Berkshire Hills seems to be gaining acceptance.

Berkshire residents — and visitors — refer to the area variously as "Berkshire County," as simply "Berkshire," and as "the Berkshires," actually a 20th-century term created to publicize the area. This book does likewise.

To my parents

"*Then all my gladsome way along . . .*"
– Johann J. Schütz (1640–1690)

TABLE OF CONTENTS

HIKES & WALKS

SOUTH COUNTY

CENTRAL COUNTY

NORTH COUNTY

WALKS FOR THE BLIND AND DISABLED 201

APPENDICES

LIST OF MAPS

Maps & Page Numbers   **U.S.Geological
                                           Survey
                                           Quadrangle**

SOUTH COUNTY

CENTRAL COUNTY

NORTH COUNTY

WALKS FOR THE BLIND AND DISABLED

Regional map, Inside back cover

United States Geological Survey (USGS) maps are available, by quadrangles, as listed above. These do not conform to town boundaries, but are named by the distinguishing feature on each quad. The maps are available at book and sporting goods stores (see the Appendix), or from USGS, Reston, VA 22092.

MAP LEGEND

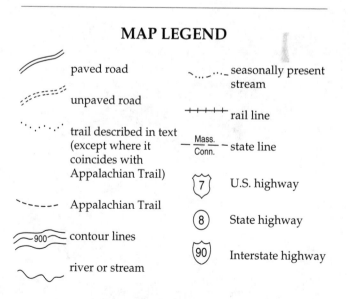

paved road

unpaved road

trail described in text (except where it coincides with Appalachian Trail)

Appalachian Trail

contour lines 900

river or stream

seasonally present stream

rail line

state line — Mass. / Conn.

U.S. highway 7

State highway 8

Interstate highway 90

PREFACE

Lauren Stevens's book takes you to most of the greatest places — at least those to which there is public access. Whether your taste runs to the easy stroll or the forced march, there's something in the Berkshires for you. Just remember, as Lauren points out: Every trail is two trails — one going and one coming back.

Walking in scenic spots is, in fact, a long-standing Berkshire tradition. During the Gilded Age, another Stevens — Romanza Stevens, a Richmond farmer — had a scheme to divert to his own pockets some of the money that was pouring into Lenox on the other side of the mountain. A small investment in stairways, ladders and bridges turned out to pay dividends. Before long, habitués of the great Berkshire "cottages" — Shadowbrook, Bellefontaine, Elm Court — were turning up at the farm, prepared to part with 25 cents apiece to make the precipitous descent into Stevens Glen.

Then as now, Lenox Mountain Brook dropped 100 feet through the cleft rock of the glen, falling freely at first before cascading noisily from pool to pool. The attraction proved serious enough to draw an average of 50 visitors a day on a fair weekend — "coaching parties to the Glen were quite the thing," a Pittsfield historian reported in 1936.

But Stevens's luck ran out shortly after the turn of the century. The trolley car was in, and the lines did not run near the Glen. Suddenly off the beaten track, Stevens Glen was soon forgotten.

Today, getting off the beaten track is one the main points of the Berkshires (the others aren't worth mentioning here). The region has obvious roadside charisma, but its true charms — such as the waterfall in Stevens Glen — reveal themselves only to the walker.

Stevens Glen is freely accessible today, thanks to the generosity of the Pryor family of Richmond, who in 1995 gave the land to the Berkshire Natural Resources Council. The Council, in turn, commissioned Peter Jensen of Great Barrington to create a trail into this lovely and fragile place.

Though this trail was finished too late to be included in this volume, we are happy to report that it stands with the best short walks in the Berkshires.*

And short trips to fine places are the hallmark of Berkshire hiking. To be sure, the long-range hiker can take some splendid walks here. The Appalachian Trail runs the entire length of the county, and there are many other terrific outings described in these pages that should take the better part of a day — Mt. Alander to Bash Bish Falls is just one of the standouts.

But it's those short walks or hikes, tucked into an hour or two between other appointments, that in so many ways define the character of the Berkshires, and the best joys of living or visiting here.

If Mount Greylock is too much to bite off, try the rewarding trip up Monument Mountain. Stockbridge's Ice Glen and Williamstown's Stone Hill offer wild and pastoral experiences, respectively, barely a stone's throw from the village centers. The view from Bartholomew's Cobble in Sheffield is not half-bad, and no one ever went wrong with a ramble through Gould Meadows down to Stockbridge Bowl.

And while there are undeniable rewards to hiking long and hard to get to a lonely and windswept spot high above anyone who might help you if you slip and break your ankle, there is likewise a warm and happy feeling to arriving at a quiet lake or comfortable summit whose qualities have been sufficient to attract genteel explorers for a century or more.

Because let's face it: Wilderness is not the Berkshires. The region has its wild places, but by and large it's a placid landscape shaped heavily by the hand of mankind. The Berkshires' most lovely natural features may be off the beaten track, but they're not necessarily far from it. You just have to

---

*To find Stevens Glen, take Rte. 183 south from the center of Lenox. Just past Tanglewood's gates at a fork in the road, turn right up the hill toward Richmond. After passing Olivia's Overlook at the summit, turn left down a road marked Lenox Branch. Approximately three-quarters of a mile down the hill on your right, you'll see a parking pull-off at the trailhead.

know where to look, which is why we're lucky to have this book.

It's also to the great benefit of the Berkshires that a corps of private conservation groups has for many years been working to protect the best of these hills and valleys. Along with the Resources Council, we have The Trustees of Reservations and Massachusetts Audubon Society, The Nature Conservancy and the Appalachian Trail Conference, local land trusts and venerable organizations such as Stockbridge's Laurel Hill Association. In combination with those lands protected by various state conservation agencies, over 120,000 acres in the Berkshires are forever saved.

Tad Ames, Director
Berkshire Natural Resources Council
20 Bank Row
Pittsfield, Massachusetts 01201
413-499-0596

INTRODUCTION

Whether you want to amble in an afternoon through an azalea grove or take a strenuous day hike with sweeping vistas of five states, it's tough to beat Berkshire County. For variety and tradition, few areas in this country offer prospects as rich as those of the western end of Massachusetts. Some of the routes described in this book move you inward, toward contemplation and quiet. As Henry David Thoreau said of the Bellows Pipe, his trail to the summit of Mt. Greylock, "It seemed a road for the pilgrim to enter upon who would climb to the gates of heaven." Other routes, perhaps beside brooks dropping for hundreds of feet or along rocky ridges fringed with fir, make you want to shout with joy. And through them all you absorb the rhythms that previous generations have trod, an at-oneness with ancients known and unknown, famous and infamous.

These descriptions overflow into neighboring states and counties because Berkshire's mountainous boundaries — the Taconics, Greens, Hoosacs, and Litchfield Hills — themselves offer prime areas to get out and enjoy the out-of-doors under your own locomotion. The Berkshire region can test the limbs and meet the curiosities of daily walkers in infinite ways. This little book is content to list many of the best: 39 walks and 17 hikes, together with brief descriptions of 21 towns and cities in which they mostly take place.

A Few Definitions and Limitations

Walks are easier and less exerting than *Hikes*, not necessarily because they are shorter but because they involve less up and down. Several walks in this book are longer than some of the hikes. Although hike descriptions are more or less commensurate with hike lengths, walk descriptions are more idiosyncratic. They will all get you there, but some linger longer on the details of nature or culture.

Each description tells you the *length in miles* of the outing. Each hike description gives you *elapsed time*, on the grounds that you are more likely to wear a watch than a pedometer. A warning accompanies these figures, given in hours and minutes (1:37): you should add at least 20 minutes per hour, because minutes in the book include only travel time, not time to look at views, at historic artifacts, for the best way to ford a brook, or for an obscure blaze. Or for taking a rest. The times were measured by energetic folks, unencumbered by packs, papooses, or wandering puppies.

Most of the hikes are in the woods or on mountain ridges, as are some of the walks. Of the rest, most of the walks are primarily on gravel roads. Many pass cultural sites of significance. The text hints at some cross-country skiing and road bicycling possibilities. For more on biking, pick up Lew Cuyler's *Bike Rides in the Berkshire Hills*.

This walking book is *not* a guide to the *extended hiking trails* in and near the county, although sections that you happen to pass over while following these routes are described. For further information, see the Appendix. The Appalachian Mtn. Club and the Taconic Hiking Club publish guides to the Appalachian Trail and Taconic Crest Trail, respectively. Christopher J. Ryan has published a guide to the Taconic Trail System. See the Bibliography for these and other pertinent guides.

The trails in this book are marked by *blazes*. A blaze is a daub of paint, at about eye level usually, directly on a tree or rock or on wood or metal attached to a tree or driven into the ground, that marks a trail. A common route for two trails may be blazed with two colors. Two blazes, one above the other, signal a sharp turn or other unusual circumstance ahead. In this county the north-south long trails are blazed white, including the Appalachian Trail; side trails to them are blazed blue; trails that don't connect to the long trails are blazed orange . . . with some local exceptions.

The purpose of this book is to pass on information on day walks and hikes accurate as of the time I explored each of these routes, to reassure you that you are indeed on the right trail, and to encourage you — because the most important thing I learned from researching this book is that even when the weather is a bit uncertain, the distance seems a little far, you've got other things to do, or you're not feeling quite 100%, going out will always make you glad.

Glad because walking is good exercise for everyone. I hope this book helps you determine which distances and degrees of difficulty are healthiest for you. Glad because the scenery varies from serene to breathtaking and there is no better way to see it than to get yourself there under your own power, true personal empowerment. Most of what you will be looking at you cannot reach by car; for the rest, driving to it is no substitute for becoming a part of it. Glad because you and I need to rediscover periodically in a civilized grandeur like Berkshire where we have come from and perhaps discover some insight into where we are going.

But you already know these things.

Thanks

Special thanks to those people who provided information and to those who have been hiking and walking companions, including county residents Robert K. Buckwalter, Henry N. Flynt, Paul Karabinos, Christopher Niebuhr, Bernice O'Brien, George Osgood, Robert J. Redington (who authored the section on guided trails for the blind), Robert Spencer, Edgar and Piri Taft, George S. Wislocki, Reinhard A. Wobus, and Alice Sedgwick Wohl.

Whit Griswold's *Berkshire Trails for Walking and Ski Touring*, now out of print, introduced me to several previously unknown venues. The publishers and I thank him for making his text available as a resource. Jonathan Sternfield's *The Berkshire Book: A Complete Guide* supplied information and maps for several sections of this book.

Several of these hikes first appeared in an earlier version in *The Advocate* newspaper in Williamstown. I spent a fine morning hiking Shaker Mtn. with John Manners, who rediscovered the site, researched its history, and led the Boy Scouts in laying out the trail. Deborah Burns made stylistic suggestions on this manuscript. Robert D. Hatton, Jr., county trail coordinator for the Department of Environmental Management, reviewed the material. If you spot an error, blame me — and then, please, let me know about it or other improvements in care of the publisher, so we can correct the next edition.

All the hikes and some of the walks were revisited for this new edition. As well, it includes information you, the walker, have suggested.

HOW TO USE THIS BOOK

This book tries its best to be accurate and helpful. Neither the author nor the publisher can be responsible beyond that effort. Many things, both natural and manmade, are subject to change and out of the author's control. And, with the best intentions, errors are possible.

Key Terms, Important Names, Abbreviations

The word "facilities," as used here, refers to man-made structures that could be of convenience to the walker. As an example of facilities, the descriptions differentiate between flush toilets and outhouses — what the state calls pit toilets. The initials "HQ" refer to headquarters for either state-owned or privately owned properties opened to the public. The difference between *Hikes* and *Walks* is explained in the Introduction, as is the term "blazes," and how to read them.

"AMC" refers to the Appalachian Mtn. Club, the hiking and environmentally oriented not-for-profit organization that is concessionaire in Bascom Lodge on the summit of Mt. Greylock. It is related to but not the same as the Appalachian Trail Conference, the group of local organizations that maintain the Appalachian Trail (AT), the foot trail from Georgia to Maine. The AT passes through Berkshire County. Some of the hikes and walks in the book use parts of the footpath. While much of the AT in the county runs across state land, the National Park Service has purchased stretches of land to create an AT corridor to protect the trail.

Another not-for-profit environmental organization, the Massachusetts Audubon Society, a separate entity from the public National Audubon Society, owns and maintains two sanctuaries in Berkshire, both of which are described in the text. Another major landowner is also private, the Trustees of Reservations (TTOR), a statewide group originally founded as analogous to a public library: a resource available to the public for beautiful and historic places. Four hikes or walks in this book take place on their land.

Yet another private group, the New England Forestry Foundation, owns the Dorothy Frances Rice Sanctuary. Hikes and walks also cross the lands of Berkshire School in Sheffield, and Buxton School and the Clark Art Institute in Williamstown. Three hikes cross land belonging to Williams College, in Williamstown. Walkers in the county owe a debt to many private landowners who willingly share the enjoyment of special places.

Walkers are indebted, as well, to numerous groups who lay out, maintain, and map trails, such as the Appalachian Trail Conference, Berkshire School, the state's Division of Forests and Parks, the Green Mtn. Club, the Williams (College) Outing Club, and the Taconic Hiking Club of New York — which is responsible for the Taconic Crest Trail (TCT).

Additional Maps

To find some of the not-so-obvious corners of the county, a supplement to regular road maps is advisable. One is *Jimapco Map C12, Berkshire County, MA*, 3rd edition, $3.95. It is available in bookstores, drugstores, and newspaper stores or from Jimapco, Box 1137, Clifton Park, NY 12065; 1-800-MAPS 123. A lovely road map is also available from the County Surveyors' Office, Bowes Building, Park Square, Pittsfield, MA 01201. Our *List of Maps* indicates the U.S. Geological Survey quadrangle(s) for each hike and walk. These maps are available at bookstores and sporting goods stores. They provide the base for virtually all county maps.

Organization

Following a generally accepted tradition, this book is organized in three parts: South, Central, and North County, as shown on the adjacent map. That should be a help in locating the hikes and walks closest to you. Here is a plug, however: try some farther removed. Differences exist, interesting in their own right and helpful in defining the characteristics of the walks with which you are most familiar.

NORTH COUNTY
Adams (Population: 9,270)
Cheshire (3,500)
Clarksburg (1,722)
Florida (735)
New Ashford (226)
North Adams (14,410)
Savoy (683)
Williamstown (8,368)

CENTRAL COUNTY
Becket (1,640)
Dalton (7,077)
Hancock (640)
Hinsdale (2,085)
Lanesborough (3,029)
Lenox (5,661)
Peru (810)
Pittsfield (43,981)
Richmond (1,784)
Washington (600)
Windsor (862)

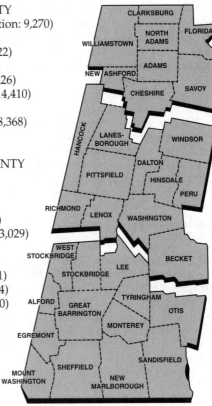

SOUTH COUNTY
Alford (429)
Egremont (1,042)
Great Barrington (7,616)
Lee (5,760)
Monterey (841)
Mount Washington (146)

New Marlborough (1,021)
Otis (1,073)
Sandisfield (866)
Sheffield (3,327)
Stockbridge (2,396)
Tyringham (600)
West Stockbridge (1,475)

TRANSPORTATION

Getting to the Berkshire

BY CAR

From Manhattan: Take the Major Deegan Expressway or the Henry Hudson Parkway to the Saw Mill River Parkway, then proceed north on one of the most beautiful roadways in the world, the Taconic State Parkway. For southern Berkshire, exit the Taconic at "Hillsdale, Claverack, Rte. 23" and follow 23 east, toward Hillsdale and on to Great Barrington. For Stockbridge, Lee, and Lenox, proceed up Rte. 7. For Williamstown and all of northern Berkshire, you might want to proceed farther up the Taconic and exit at Rte. 295. Follow 295 east to Rte. 22. Take 22 north to Rte. 43, then follow Rte. 43 through Hancock to Williamstown.

From New Jersey, Pennsylvania, and south: If local color is high on your list or you'd rather ramble northward, Rte. 22 north is a good choice, and you can pick it up as far south as Armonk or Bedford in Westchester County, New York. Rte. 22 is a road still proud of its diners: of particular note is the Red Rooster in Brewster, just north of I-684's end. Further upstate on Rte. 22, turn right at Hillsdale on Rte. 23 east toward Great Barrington, Rte. 20 to Pittsfield, and Rte. 43 to Williamstown. For the most direct route from New Jersey, Pennsylvania, and south, take the New York Thruway to I-84 east; at the Taconic Parkway, turn north, following instructions "From Manhattan."

From Connecticut and/or the New York metro area: Rte. 7 north was an early stagecoach thoroughfare to Berkshire, and you join the same trail at Danbury, via I-684 and I-84. Driving up Rte. 7, you'll wend your way along the beautiful Housatonic River, north through New Milford, Kent, and Canaan and into Massachusetts through Ashley Falls (an especially good ride for picnics and antiques). To arrive in southeastern Berkshire, Rte. 8 is a quick and scenic drive as it follows the Farmington River north.

BERKSHIRE ACCESS

Using Tanglewood (on the Stockbridge — Lenox line) as the Berkshire reference point, the following cities are this close.

CITY	TIME	MILES
Albany	1 hr	50
Boston	2½ hrs	135
Bridgeport	2 hrs	110
Danbury	1¾ hrs	85
Hartford	1½ hrs	70
Montreal	5 hrs	275
New Haven	2½ hrs	115
New York City	3 hrs	150
Philadelphia	4½ hrs	230
Providence	2½ hrs	125
Springfield	¾ hr	35
Waterbury	1½ hrs	75
Washington, DC	7 hrs	350
Worcester	1¾ hrs	90

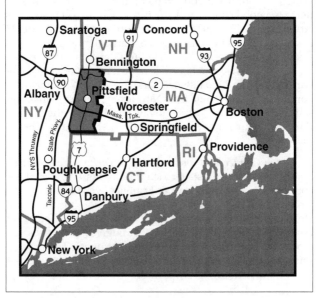

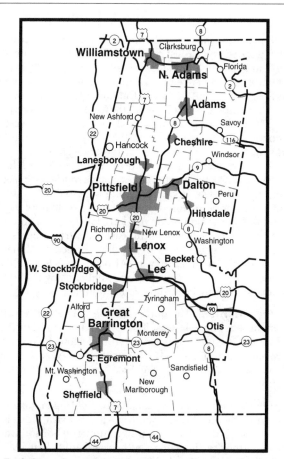

Berkshire County is 56 miles south to north, from Sheffield to Williamstown. Because of the mountain ranges that run along this route, east-west travel across the county remains much more difficult, with all the county's east-west routes (2 in the north; 9, midcounty; and 23 in the south) being tricky drives in freezing or snowy weather.

From Boston and east: The scenic Massachusetts Turnpike is the quickest and easiest route west to south Berkshire and Pittsfield. From Boston, there's no better bet, especially as tolls at the western end have been dropped. For the best route to Otis Ridge, Butternut Basin, and Catamount ski areas, you can leave the turnpike at Exit 3 west of the Connecticut River, take Rte. 202 south to Rte. 20 west, and pick up Rte. 23 west at Woronoco. Most people stay on the turnpike right into the Berkshires, exiting either at Lee or West Stockbridge.

A less rapid but more colorful route westward from Boston is Rte. 20, which cuts across southern Massachusetts, connecting with Lee. If you're coming west to the Berkshires from more northern latitudes, Rte. 9 from Northampton is a splendid drive, a high road with long lovely vistas and few towns. Still farther to the north, eastern entry to Berkshire County can be gained by driving the spectacular Mohawk Trail, originally an Indian byway. Also known as Rte. 2, this is the most direct way to North Adams, Williamstown, and the ski slopes at Jiminy Peak and Brodie Mountain.

From Hartford: The quickest route is I-91 north to the Massachusetts Turnpike west. Then proceed as in the directions for Massachusetts Turnpike travel from Boston. A slower but more pleasant drive is Rte. 44 west, up through Avon, Norfolk, and Canaan, where you take Rte. 7 north into Berkshire County.

From Montreal and Albany: Leaving Canada, take I-87 (known as "the Northway") south to Albany. Exit at either Rte. 7 to Rte. 2 toward Williamstown, or continue on I-87 south and I-90 east (they're the same south of Albany). Exit I-90 in Austerlitz, NY (Exit B-3), or continue east onto the Massachusetts Turnpike and exit at Lee (exit 2).

BY BUS
Please note: Schedules and prices are subject to change. We advise that you call ahead to check.

From Manhattan (3.5 hours): Bonanza (800-556-3815) serves the Berkshires out of New York City's *Port Authority*

Bus Terminal (212-564-8484) at 40th St. between 8th and 9th Aves. Tickets may be purchased at the Greyhound ticket windows (800-231-2222), near 8th Ave. Several buses a day. Boarding is down the escalators at the center of the terminal, and then to the right, usually at Gate 13. Berkshire locales marked with an asterisk (*) are Flag Stops, where you must wave to the bus driver in order to be picked up.

Berkshire Phone Numbers for New York Buses

Canaan, CT .... Canaan Pharmacy, Main St.
860-824-5481

Gt. Barrington .... Bill's Pharmacy, 362 Main St.
413-528-1590

Hillsdale, NY .... *Junction Rtes. 22 & 23
800-556-3815

Lee .... McClelland Drugs, 43 Main St.
413-243-0135

Lenox .... Lenox News & Variety, 39 Housatonic St.
413-637-2815

New Ashford .... *Entrance to Brodie Mt. Ski Area, Rte. 7
800-556-3815

Pittsfield .... Bus Terminal, 57 S. Church St.
413-442-4451

Sheffield .... *Bank of Boston, Rte. 7
800-556-3815

S. Egremont .... *Gaslight Store
800-556-3815

Stockbridge .... Information Booth, Main St.
800-556-3815

Williamstown .... The Williams Inn, 1090 Main St.
413-458-2665

From Boston (3.5 hours): *Bonanza* and *Greyhound* serve the Berkshires from Boston out of the *Greyhound Terminal* at 10 St. James Ave. (800-231-2222). *Peter Pan/Trailways* runs daily to Pittsfield and North Adams-Williamstown out of the Trailways Terminal at South Station. Berkshire-bound passengers change buses at Springfield. Call 800-343-9999 for prices and schedules.

Berkshire Phone Numbers for Boston Buses

Lee .... McClelland Drugs, 43 Main St.
413-243-0135
Lenox .... Lenox News & Variety, 39 Housatonic St.
413-637-2815
Pittsfield .... Bus Terminal, 57 S. Church St.
413-442-4451
Williamstown .... The Williams Inn, 1090 Main St.
413-458-2665

From Hartford (1.75 hours): The *Greyhound Line* runs two buses to Pittsfield daily, at 11:15 a.m. and 4:20 p.m., from the *Greyhound Terminal* at 409 Church St., Hartford (860-522-9267).

From Montreal (6 hours): *Greyhound* runs south to the Albany Greyhound Terminal. Connect to Pittsfield as noted below.

From Albany (1 hour): *Bonanza* runs two buses daily from Albany to Pittsfield. *Greyhound* runs one bus daily.

BY TRAIN
From Manhattan: You can ride at the commuter rate, a fraction of the regular, if you get off at Dover Plains, NY. *Amtrak* (800-USA-RAIL or 800-872-7245) can also help you get to the Berkshires. Their turboliner from Grand Central Station runs frequently and smoothly along the Hudson River, a splendid ride. For southern Berkshire, stay aboard till Hudson, NY, a river town recently restored; for northern Berkshire, carry on to Rensselaer, NY. For travel connections from Dover Plains, Hudson, or Rensselaer to the Berkshires, see "By Taxi or Limousine."

From Boston: Amtrak may continue to run a single train daily through the Berkshires, starting from Boston's South Station. To find the Pittsfield shelter: take West St. west past the Hilton; at the first light, turn right onto Center St.; take the next right onto Depot St.; the shelter is on the left. Anyone boarding the train in Pittsfield must purchase tickets on the train. The round-trip ticket prices vary, depending on time of travel and seat availability. Private compartments are available.

From Montreal: Amtrak runs one train daily from Montreal through Albany. There is no same-day train connection from this run to the Berkshires; see "By Limousine or Taxi"; or see "By Bus."

From Albany: Amtrak may continue a single daily Pittsfield-bound train from the Albany/Rensselaer Depot on East St. (2 miles from downtown Albany), stopping at Pittsfield's Depot St. shelter (see directions above under "From Boston").

BY PLANE

If you own a small airplane or decide to charter one, you can fly directly to the Berkshires, landing at Gt. Barrington, Pittsfield, or N. Adams airports.

From New York City: Feeling rich, traveling high with some friends, or riding on the corporate account? There are several charter air companies in the metropolitan New York area that will fly you from La Guardia, JFK, or other airports near New York to any of the Berkshire airports. Charters currently flying these routes include:

> Aircraft Charter Group 800-553-3590
> Chester Charter, Chester, CT 800-752-6371
> Long Island Airways 800-645-9572

and from Westchester County:

> Panorama (White Plains airport) 914-328-9800
>   if calling from New York City: 718-507-9800
> Richmor Aviation . . . 800-331-6101 or 518-828-9461

From Boston: There are several charter flight companies that fly from Beantown to Berkshire. Some of those you can try are:

> Bird Airfleet 508-372-6566
> Wiggins Airways . . . . 617-762-5690 Ext. #251

From Hartford: Bradley Airport outside Hartford handles numerous domestic and international airlines, so you can fly to Bradley from nearly anywhere. From there, charter air service to the Berkshires is available through the companies listed under "From Boston" or through the Berkshire County companies listed below.

From Albany: Albany is terminus for a substantial volume of domestic jet traffic and, being less than an hour from the Berkshires by car, is the closest you can get to these hills by jet. Charter connector flights from Albany to the Berkshires are available through Signature Flight Support (518-869-0253) or through the Berkshire County companies listed below.

In Berkshire County: There are two aviation companies in Berkshire County which operate air taxi service to just about any other northeastern airport.

Berkshire Aviation . . . . Gt. Barrington Airport
413-528-1010 or -528-1061
Esposito Flying Service . . . Harriman & West Airport,
N. Adams, 413-663-3330

LODGING AND DINING

Berkshire offers a host of possibilities for lodging and dining, from the humble to the luxurious. The popularity of the area as a tourist destination means that those who want to visit in the high seasons (summer and fall) must plan ahead. Lodging reservations are particularly important. We recommend two approaches to finding a place to stay and deciding where to eat. *The Berkshire Book: A Complete Guide*, by Jonathan Sternfield and Lauren R. Stevens, from the publishers of this hiking guide, is a thoroughly researched travel book, covering not only lodging and dining, but culture, recreation, shopping and many other topics as well. *The New York Times* said its recommendations were "right on the money." It is available from bookstores throughout the United States or from the publisher (Berkshire House, 480 Pleasant St., Lee, MA 01238; $17.95). Or you can call the Berkshire Visitors Bureau (413-443-9186) to ask for their package of brochures about lodging and dining possibilities. Both *The Berkshire Book* and the Visitors Bureau provide telephone numbers for Chamber of Commerce and other lodging reservations services.

Jonathan Sternfield's *The Berkshire Book* actually reviews restaurants and food purveyors, and you might enjoy seeing whether your opinions harmonize with his. Don't forget that one of the best dining possibilities for hikers and walkers is the well-planned picnic along the trail. Berkshire offers several traditional country general stores where you can get provisions, or, if you like, elegant gourmet picnics-to-go can be ordered from many of the area's upscale grocers and caterers.

SAFETY

Walking and hiking are two of the safest and healthiest activities you might engage in. Compared to driving a car, working in the kitchen, cutting firewood . . . your chances of being injured in the slightest are extremely small. That is the way it should be: walking should be a worry-free, non-competitive, relaxing avocation. Walking doesn't even lead to pimples.

This section ought to stop right here, without borrowing trouble. Nevertheless, after wandering around the county for several decades, I have accumulated a small amount of wisdom that could, conceivably, save you an equal amount of pain.

A Few Basic Rules

I want to share with you some things you probably already know but of which you may need to be reminded. I'll do it as succinctly as possible. They are all summed up in rule number one.

1. Take a few minutes before you go out to think through what you're going to do.
2. Carry water. You can't be certain even of lovely mountain brooks.
3. Wear comfortable, stout shoes — not sneakers or running shoes.
4. Remember that it may get warmer or cooler, especially on ridges.
5. Always tell someone where you are going.
6. Signs and blazes are constructions of man and cannot always be trusted. Leave the cares of civilization behind but take along a map such as the ones in this book, a compass, and a watch.
7. Stay on the trail.
8. Do not leave any trash.

These rules and this book ought to get you where you want to go . . . and back.

A special few words for newcomers to Berkshire. Welcome! Are there any dangers lurking on the roadside or in the woods? Yes, a few. In the extreme southwestern part of the county rattlesnakes live on the rock outcroppings. This book warns you on which trails they might be encountered. *They* warn you if you are getting too near. Should you get bitten you have time to get to help from just about anywhere described here, which you should do in an unhurried but deliberate manner.

You might see a bear, which will usually run from you, especially if you make some noise. Do not try to approach a bear.

Some people are allergic to some kinds of bees. If so, they should carry a bee sting kit. In 30 years of walking in Berkshire I have never seen a rattler or been stung by a bee (in the woods).

Poison ivy exists in openings, at lower elevations. I have asked Alison Kolesar, who drew the lovely illustrated  maps for this book, to draw poison ivy leaves, so that you will know what to avoid. Ticks that carry Lyme disease are rife in Connecticut and the eastern end of Massachusetts. Perhaps over the next few years they will move out this way. Tuck your trousers into your socks and inspect yourself after outings. Because of the terrain, storms can arrive without much warning — more of a potential problem in the winter than the summer. Take along extra clothes.

Hunters

Stay out of the woods and even off gravel roads during hunting season. Check at the local town hall for the dates, because Massachusetts, Connecticut, New York, and Vermont each has different seasons and each state has a variety of seasons for different animals and weapons. In general, be on the alert from mid-November through mid-December, especially for shotgun deer season, which attracts the most two-legged participants.

Automobiles

Walk against traffic on roads. Wear reflective clothing at dusk. If you are parking your car, be certain the shoulder is firm. Lock your car. If you don't like to take your keys with you for fear of losing them, remember that losing your keys, while annoying, is ultimately less of a problem than losing your car.

Weather

Mark Twain, who ought to know because he summered in Tyringham, said of local weather, if you don't like it, wait five minutes. He exaggerated. Berkshire weather does grow less predictable as you gain elevation, however, and summer thunderstorms or winter snow squalls can come out of nowhere. Normally you would expect county weather to be affected by the area's proximity (less than 150 mi.) to the ocean. Because of the hills, however, this area is controlled more by the prevailing westerly wind. Thus winters are colder and summers are cooler than either east or south of Berkshire.

Average Temperature
October   49.3
January   21.2
April   44.3
July   68.3
Average precipitation
Snow   70"
Rain   36.14"
Total   43.14"

Clothing

It is not necessary to invest heavily in trendy clothing, but consider the likelihood that the weather will change on your walk. Wear layers. If that means taking a small pack, well, that pack can also carry camera, snack, small first-aid kit, extra socks, and rain gear. A pair of well-broken-in, comfortable boots or shoes is your single most important piece of equipment. These shoes are worth some extra time, applying Neatsfoot oil or waterproofing. Wear wool socks.

Trail Indicators

Most trails in the county are well marked, which means that the next blaze is generally visible from the previous one. Don't keep going if you run out of blazes. Dry creek beds look deceptively like paths — sometimes they are, but sometimes they aren't. While a blowdown can disrupt a path, forcing a temporary detour, thanks to the hard work of many volunteers the trails described in this book are kept in good shape. So if what you're on doesn't seem like a trail anymore, turn back until you find hard evidence that you're going the right way.

Useful Items in the Woods

Water, map, compass, jackknife, matches, and small flashlight. As well as providing stability and a little extra push when needed, a walking stick can check the ground ahead for dampness and fend off the blows of Little John, should you run into him while crossing the Housatonic on a log. Bring a book to read while leisurely soaking up the ambiance.

First Aid

"Off" is apparently one of the few insect repellents that really work; Avon's "Skin So Soft" is also effective, even though it was intended for other purposes. Some folks swear by Cutters' for mosquitoes and black flies. What you don't wear — such as shampoos, perfume, aftershave lotion — can also be important. If you make yourself smell like a flower, you are likely to attract bugs. Your first-aid kit should include a general purpose ointment and band-aids large enough to cover a blister on your foot.

Avoid poison ivy, bees, Lyme ticks, if there be any, rattlesnakes, and bears.

After reading all this, you'll know as much as the natives.

BERKSHIRE HISTORY

Both natural history and social history in Berkshire are tales of ups and downs. Looking at both from the end of the 20th century, you may feel some past time was better than the present, but it ain't necessarily so. The county testifies that geography, for all our veneer of civilization, is still destiny. And this county, now, maintains a delicate balance of being close to but not too close to the Boston-Washington megalopolis that holds down the East Coast. It is an accessible hinterland. It has the position and the resources to rise up into the future.

Six hundred million years ago the area was down, under the ocean, which was at work forming the rocks. It was warm and wet, with sandy beaches and clear, shallow waters. The lapping waves built up beaches that turned to sandstone, which in turn metamorphosed into quartzite — the erosion-resistant backbone of many of the county's ridges. Shelled marine animals built coral reefs, which calcified into limestone. The deposits of this alkaline agent, mined on the side of Mt. Greylock in Adams, protect the area from the worst ravages of acid precipitation today. Some of that limestone was crystalized into marble, snowy chunks of which grace the hiking trails and can be inspected at the Natural Bridge in Clarksburg. Muddy off-shore sediments settled to form shales and then schists, crystalline rocks that fracture cleanly. The bands of granite that run through the southern part of the county antedate the metamorphic rock.

The continents began to shift, in response to subterranean pressure. At a speed of about an inch a year over 150 million years, the land masses that would one day be North America, Africa, and Europe moved towards each other, closing the proto-Atlantic ocean. Several arcs of offshore volcanic islands were shoved onto the continent by a series of slow but cataclysmic collisions known as the Taconic Orogeny (Taconic mountain building). The entire continental shelf was squeezed into a series of folds, the monumental forerunners of the Appalachian Range. The bases of these mountains, some Himalayan in height, must have just about filled Berkshire, when the county reached for the sky. Then the continents began to pull apart, as they are still doing.

As soon as mountains were stacked up, the process of erosion began. Rain fell, forming rivers that still drain these hills, but in those days more vigorously carving a landscape unrooted by vegetation. Not only water but wind sculpted Berkshire hills, raging unbroken by trees and shrubs. The rugged landscape was tamed, waiting only for plants to soften it.

Less than two million years ago the first of a succession of four ice sheets ground down in response to a cooling climate. These mile-high glaciers brought debris, gravel and rocks, which they deposited around the nubbins of mountains that remained. Glacial lakes covered most of north county and a good portion of the south. Because the Hoosac Valley was preglacial, once the melt set in, the Hoosic River returned to flowing across the north-south path of the ice. This and the Upper Ammonoosuc in New Hampshire are the odd rivers in New England that flow from southeast to northwest. Nor were the beds of the Housatonic or Westfield much altered. The Farmington River ran up against a load of glacial trash that turned its general southerly course in Connecticut.

The ice withdrew as recently as 10,000 years ago. Vegetation and then wildlife followed its retreating edge. Perhaps a few of the earliest North American inhabitants, having boated or walked across the land bridge from Asia, were in Berkshire to bid farewell to the ice. Gradually, the evergreen forest moved north, lingering only on the tops of the highest ridges, while the broad-leaved, deciduous forest moved in, characterized in North County by sugar maple and in the south by oak, with their associated pines, ash, beech, birch, and alder.

The rocky steepness of the county does not lend itself to leisurely flowing water and big lakes. With the exception of the southern reach of the Housatonic, which meanders in curlicues through Sheffield, Berkshire rivers retain little water and rush to their destinations. What lakes the county has, it owes to the efforts of 19th-century industrialists to create a head or a reservoir to provide a year-round flow of water for power or other manufacturing processes: Otis Reservoir, Cheshire Reservoir, Pontoosuc, Onota, and others.

Seen from above, the county presents the ridges that remain from the north-south running folds, the Taconics along the New York line, the lower end of the Green Mountains protruding over the Vermont line, the Hoosacs filling the northeast quadrant, the Southern Berkshire Plateau filling the southeast quadrant, and a line of river valleys, just to the left of center, made up of the Hoosic and Housatonic — albeit flowing in opposite directions — that meet in New Ashford.

The Greylock massif stands as a peninsula to the Taconics — as indeed it was when glacial Lake Bascom filled the Hoosac Valley up to the 1,300-ft. contour. Therefore it may be appropriate that the summit of Greylock lifts a War Memorial Tower, designed originally as a lighthouse for the Charles River estuary, bearing a beacon that can be seen by people navigating most of the county. If any man-made feature is needed to unite a geographical area so well defined topographically, it would be that tower and the roads it guards (Rtes. 2, 7, and 8).

Getting in and out and around Berkshire used to be a problem. The native Americans generally thought of the area as removed from their Hudson River homes, a hunting ground to visit in the summer. The Mahicans entered from the south or north, along the river valleys. Although the Bay Colony claimed the land early on, Bay Colony residents found it tough to surmount the Berkshire barrier to the east. Early settlers found it easier to enter along the valleys, a few Dutch infiltrating through the Taconics from New York, but especially residents from the area now known as Connecticut, up the Housatonic. Thus the county was settled from the south to the north, the earliest towns in the south dating to the first quarter of the 18th century. The main roads, railroads, and even sewer lines now follow the valleys.

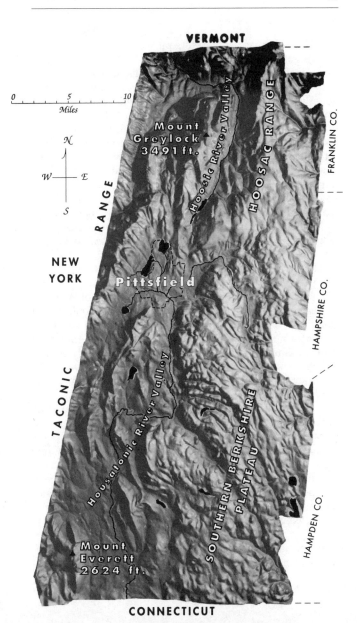

VERMONT

0   5   10
Miles

N
W — E
S

RANGE

NEW
YORK

TACONIC

Mount
Greylock
3491 ft.

Hoosic River Valley

HOOSAC RANGE

FRANKLIN CO.

Pittsfield

HAMPSHIRE CO.

Housatonic River Valley

SOUTHERN BERKSHIRE PLATEAU

Mount
Everett
2624 ft.

HAMPDEN CO.

CONNECTICUT

The European settlers were primarily farmers, typically working the bottom lands and, as they filled up, moving up the sides of the hills. Remains of walls, cellar holes, and orchards such as you come across in your ambles remind you that even what seem now lofty ridges were at one time home, especially for those who made their living grazing cattle or merino sheep. In Stockbridge, the English Society for the Propagation of the Gospel in Foreign Parts set up an Indian mission, which gradually acceded to the land hunger of the Europeans. By the time of the Revolution, virtually all native Americans had departed.

As a farmer installed a mill to grind his corn or saw his wood, and his neighbors came to have him do their milling, so industry followed the plough. What began as groupings to protect against French or Indian raids became trading centers. Specialty manufactures, depending on natural resources, developed, such as glass, paper, charcoal, and textiles. Even education can be seen as an industry depending on natural resources. After all, Thoreau said of Williams College's position at the foot of Greylock: "It would be no small advantage if every college were thus located at the base of a mountain, as good at least as one well-endowed professorship . . . . Some will remember, no doubt, not only that they went to college, but that they went to the mountain." In Berkshire County, three of the four colleges and many of the secondary schools are at the base of mountains.

The opening of the Erie Canal in 1825, providing a practical means for younger residents to head west where the thick topsoil had a lot fewer glacial stones than that of Berkshire, drained the county of human resources. One by one lights winked out on the sidehill farms. Whereas by the middle of the century three-quarters of the trees had been stripped for pasture land or to feed the insatiable maws of the railroad, the county has been revegetating for 150 years. In Berkshire that ratio is inverted today. The county is three-quarters wooded, which is why coyotes, bear, beaver, turkeys, and even moose are returning to join the populous deer and smaller animals.

The most important industrial event in the county's history happened in 1886, when William Stanley linked 25 shops along the main street of Great Barrington in the world's first commercial electric system. That, in turn, drew the General Electric Co. to Stanley's shop in Pittsfield. GE has been here ever since, although greatly diminished by successive waves of layoffs and corporate buy-outs in the past decades. The second most important industrial event was the opening of the Hoosac Tunnel, at 4.75 miles the longest bore in the world in 1875, breaking through the Berkshire barrier for direct train service in the North County from Boston to Albany.

Yet even in the heady days when industry was king — the population of Pittsfield growing from 25,000 to 58,000 in the first 60 years of the 20th century — second homes, tourism, and culture were already crown princes. In the Gilded Age that ended the 19th century, wealthy men collected great estates and built luxury palaces, known as "cottages," some 75 in Lenox and Stockbridge. Major literary figures toured the county: Emerson, Melville, Hawthorne, Holmes, Thoreau, Wharton, Twain. . . . Some settled here. Actors, musicians, and artists followed, and are still following.

As the county now, somewhat painfully, recognizes that industries will never again be what they were through World War II, it is coming to rely on a service economy to which, at least, it is no stranger. Filled with fine educational institutions, public and private, with museums and musicians, with art and artifacts to grace the green walls installed infinitely earlier by nature, Berkshire now boasts streams that are cleaner and woods that are thicker than since farms and industry first came to these garrison hills. And the hills retain a plentiful supply of ground water, likely to become increasingly important to the future of this area.

Berkshire has now, as it has had since the ice left, an indigenous population that cares deeply for the land, witness the many towns in the county that have long had zoning, have now established land trusts, and are considering land use countywide. Berkshire residents listen attentively at town meetings to discussions of protecting ridges and aquifers, saving farm land, and cleaning up hazardous waste. Little litter mars the many paths. Whether driving its roads or walking its trails, you will soon get the message that this land is cared for.

SOUTH COUNTY

MOUNT WASHINGTON

Mt. Washington, the smallest town by population in the Commonwealth of Massachusetts, has 146 residents. It contains 6,500 acres of state land — like the towns of Washington, Savoy, and New Ashford, about half the town is state owned. Perched at a 2,000-ft. elevation, like Savoy and Windsor, it is a town formed by its topography. The town may have been settled first by Dutch moving east from the Hudson River as early as 1692. That would make it the oldest town in Berkshire, but the point is disputed. In any case, the mountain men who lived there about 1730 preferred to consider themselves Bay Colony residents, where individuals owned their land, rather than subject to the feudal tenure of the Hudson Valley. Hudson lord Robert Livingston sent a party onto the mountain in 1755 to extract rents deeded him by the governor of New Amsterdam. A skirmish broke out. Pioneer William Race, for whom Mt. Race and Race Brook were probably named, was killed. In 1761 Livingston's men burned six homes in Mt. Washington. In spite of the fact that the town was incorporated in 1781, the dispute continued until the New York-Massachusetts boundary was settled in 1787.

In the 1840s and '50s inhabitants earned their living by cutting trees and making charcoal; later, they farmed potatoes; now they drive down off their mountain to work at jobs elsewhere. The scenery is spectacular — a phrase not often used even in a book limited to the best of Berkshire. What a place to begin!

Camping

Part of the charm of Mt. Washington is the absence of any tourist facilities. There is a state-owned cabin on the trail between the two peaks of Alander that can be used on a first-come, first-served basis. The primitive camping area on the Alander Trail is lovely for tenting (no facilities). Camping is available at the New York end of the two-state Bash Bish Park, with facilities. A cabin is available to AMC members (reserved in advance) off East Rd. near Sage's Ravine. There are campsites along the AT at Sage's Ravine, Bear Rock Falls, and Race Brook; a shelter is available just north of Mt. Everett at Glen Brook.

HIKES

ALANDER MOUNTAIN / BASH BISH FALLS

7 miles (3 hours), plus 4.5 miles to complete loop

Road approaches

Take Rte. 41 S. from So. Egremont village, but turn right just past the pond, on Mt. Washington Rd. (There is a state forest sign.) After 3 mi., the road swings southerly and begins to climb to a ridge. Signs help at the intersections, but essentially head straight to the Mt. Washington State Forest HQ, on the right 9 mi. from the village. Park there. If you choose to make this a 2-car expedition, which is recommended, take the signed road right at the church (before forest HQ) to Bash Bish Falls upper (first paved) parking lot (7.5 mi.). Leave car No. 1 there; drive No. 2 back to forest HQ.

ALANDER MOUNTAIN

The extremes of this hike, Alander Mtn. and Bash Bish Falls, are remarkable by any set of criteria. The open ridge of the mountain (2,239 ft.) has a fine view west to the Catskills and, if the weather is clear, even to the tall buildings in Albany,

New York, 50 mi. north. As you hike north from the summit, continual twists in the trail reveal new views, especially the intimate one down into an uplands farm. The waters of Bash Bish Brook plunge 200 ft. at the falls, the most spectacular in Berkshire, divided partway down by a pulpit-like granite outcropping before tumbling into a pool and thence other riffles and pools downstream. (The falls are always worth seeing, although the amount of water varies considerably: most in spring and fall.)

The Alander Trail is well worn from the Mt. Washington State Forest HQ parking lot, where you can also register to use the campground. Follow W. the triangular blue blazes the state uses to mark hiking trails, across a field, into a woods and out into another field. At this point you are on what is virtually a road. At 9 min., cross a brook on a bridge and continue on the road, passing the Ashley Hill Trail, also a woods road, on your left (1 mi.).

At 18 min. you must ford a brook — you want to wear boots rather than sneakers for all hikes. Two brooks join here, with a mill foundation right. The somewhat wet trail rises moderately through hemlock forest, which gradually becomes a laurel grove, with a few birches and oaks. Old stone walls speak of a time of farms. You pass the camping area to the left at 42 min. This oak/laurel forest is distinctly different from the northern hardwood forest you see farther upcounty, characterized by a higher percentage of sugar maples. Similar spring ephemeral flowers are visible before the leaves come on the trees, however: the mottled leaves of trout lily; hepatica with its blue-pink-white blossoms and oddly shaped leaves; spring beauty, which has rose pink flowers with grasslike leaves; distinctive dutchman's breeches, with parsleylike leaves.

The woods road ends at a circle that marks as far as the warden could drive to get to the fire tower that once stood on Alander. You pass straight through, bearing left at a junction (both branches have blue blazes). Shortly you come to an ominous sign that says: "Last water during dry season," as the branch of the brook you are following begins to peter out.

You are climbing more steeply through laurel now.

At 1:13 comes the state cabin in the notch between the south and north peaks of Alander. Just beyond is a bewildering nest of signs. Turn right, scrambling up the rocks to the western summit (3 mi. from road). Note the white blazes turning sharply N. (right) but take the time to explore the area of the old fire tower footings for the different views. The major highway on which you can see traffic is Rte. 22 in New York State. Follow along the ridge line, N., with occasional opportunities to look east as well as west, between pitch pine and thick laurel. At 1:47 you take the first of several sharp descents, following white blazes mostly painted on the rocks. Hawks sail on the warm updrafts of this ridge. The deep gorge of Bash Bish is taking shape to the right; at some point you will start to hear the roar of the falls.

After you scramble down a steep incline (2:22), a junction gives a choice of routes to the falls. The route right is shorter but involves fording Bash Bish Brook and should only be used at low water (when it hasn't rained for a while). The left fork leads past some view points and down a series of hairpin turns, through large hemlocks, into the camping area (2:49) by the shower building. Follow the white dots left, down the road to the bridge.

Massachusetts purchased the 400 acres around the falls in 1924, then, during the 1960s, 4,000 acres more to make up Mt. Washington State Forest. Since New York State owns land just downstream in Copake Falls, managing the camping area, this was the first example of these two states jointly maintaining a park (a second exists at Petersburgh Pass, west of Williamstown).

Follow the gravel road upstream from the parking lot to the falls (3:09). Stone steps lead down to the most dramatic view. As you see from the signs, swimming is not allowed. Several people trying to climb the cliffs or dive into the pools have killed themselves. Rock climbing is only allowed with permission of the park ranger. The guard rails are intended to keep you on the trails. In addition to the dan-

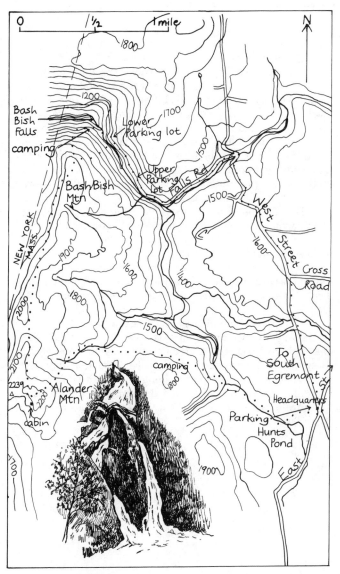

O 1/2 1 mile
N

1800

1200

Bash
Bish
Falls

Lower
Parking lot

1700

camping

1500

Upper
Parking
lot

BashBish
Mtn

Falls Rd.

1500

West

NEW YORK
MASS.

1900

1600

Street

Cross

2000

1800

1600

1400

Road

1500

To
South
Egremont

camping

1800

2200

Alander
Mtn

Headquarters

2239

Parking

cabin

2200

Hunts
Pond

East

2100

1900

St.

MT. WASHINGTON: ALANDER MTN./BASH BISH FALLS

ger of falling, rattlesnakes have been found in the vicinity.

Ten more min. take you upstream to the upper parking lot, a good place to explore the lookouts. The gorge is colonnaded with large hemlocks, some of them clinging to what appears to be nothing but rock. Like every good county cliff, Bash Bish has a myth of an Indian maiden. In this case, Bash Bish was accused of adultery and strapped into a canoe at the head of the falls as punishment. Just as the canoe was about to go over, the sun formed a halo about her head and butterflies gathered. Indians found the remains of the canoe in the pool at the bottom but not her body. The falls still say her name, if you listen closely.

This Taconic ridge on the state's border is part of the Appalachians, pushed up when the continents collided and worn down by erosion ever since. Bash Bish Brook was formed by the melting of the last glacier, 10,000 to 12,000 years ago. The quartz dike, halfway up the falls, was forced out of the earth 400 million years ago. As the sediment in the brook works in the water, it gradually destroys Bash Bish Falls.

You probably would just as soon get into No. 1 car here, as the walk by road to forest HQ is 4.5 more mi., up Falls Rd. and right on West St. A short cut, shown on old maps, along Bash Bish to the Alander Trail (3 mi. back to HQ), unfortunately crosses posted property belonging to the Mt. Washington Club. It is not blazed, signed, or completely maintained. As an alternative to 2 cars, you could leave a bicycle at Bash Bish.

MOUNT EVERETT

*Sheffield and Mt. Washington, 5.5 mile hike (2.75 hours),
plus 2 miles to complete the loop*

Road approaches

Although most of the hike is in the uplands of the town of Mt. Washington, it begins at the Berkshire School, just off Rte. 41 in Sheffield. The hike ends at a parking area about 2 mi. down the road, where the Race Brook Falls Trail comes out. So you could use 2 cars or you could walk between the beginning and end or, best idea, you could drop a bicycle off at the Race Brook trailhead. The ride back to the school on a fairly level road through lovely farm fields, looking up at the steep sides of the mountain, would be pleasant.

To get to Berkshire School, take Berkshire School Rd., appropriately enough, out of Sheffield and jog N. on Rte. 41 or, from the N., take Rtes. 23 and 41 W. from Gt. Barrington. Bear S. where 23 continues W., just after So. Egremont. The school is 3.5 mi. S. of the junction.

MOUNT EVERETT

Mt. Everett (2,602 ft.) is the outstanding peak in Berkshire County south of the Greylock massif. Although the fire tower is closed and off limits to the public, excellent views extend in most directions from the generally open summit, as well as from the Appalachian Trail (AT) to the north and especially the south. The slopes are steep on this 5.5-mi. hike and you want to wear good footgear, especially for climbing over the rock outcroppings.

As an alternative, a gravel automobile road climbs very near the summit from East St. in Mt. Washington. Call 413-528-8928 to find out when the park is open (it depends on road conditions). You could drive into the reservation to picnic at Guilder Pond and walk to the summit from the pond or from the end of the road. It would also be possible to walk N. on the AT, to be met at Berkshire School, or S. on the

AT to be met at the Race Brook trailhead, having let the car do most of the climbing.

Berkshire School (850 ft. in elevation) is most attractive, set into the side of the hills and fronted by rolling, mowed lawns. An education there comes complete with ski and hiking trails. The students maintain the Elbow Trail. You should stay on the trails, because rattlesnakes have been seen in the area.

To get to visitor parking at the school, bear right at the admissions building, past the tennis court and behind the Quonset hut. You may have to ask directions to the trail-head, but you want to walk back towards admissions. Before you get that far, follow the service road by the north end of the main building. Go past a home and straight at a hard left in the gravel road. The Elbow Trail is blazed blue, about 5 min. from parking.

The trail runs 1.2 mi. to the AT, through hemlock woods, gradually increasing in steepness. At the elbow (20 min. from the parking lot) 2 blue-blazed trails (and 1 red-blazed trail) head out. If you go generally straight on a blue, you will end up at Glen Brook. You will then have a rigorous climb, prob-ably .25 mi., without a trail, up by steep falls until you see the red roof of the Glen Brook Shelter, right. Follow the blue blazes to the AT.

A better bet at the elbow is to take a hard right on the other blue-blazed trail, which meets the AT .5 mi. farther N. (45 min. from the parking lot). In either case, turn left (S.) on the AT, blazed white. From the Elbow Trail to summit: 1.8 mi. In 20 min. from arriving on the AT you will reach the Guilder Pond Trail, entering right; then the picnic area/ parking lot on the road to the summit.

Most of the rest of the way to the summit the trail par-allels the road, until the road stops and those who drive join you on foot for the last quarter mi. Note that the AT turns left before reaching the tower, which you will do in 1:25. Over the low shrubbery, including blueberry, scrub oak, and pitch pine, you catch fine views of Alander Mtn. to the west, Mt. Frissell to the south, and, if you move around, other direc-tions as well. On a clear day, the Catskills are visible across

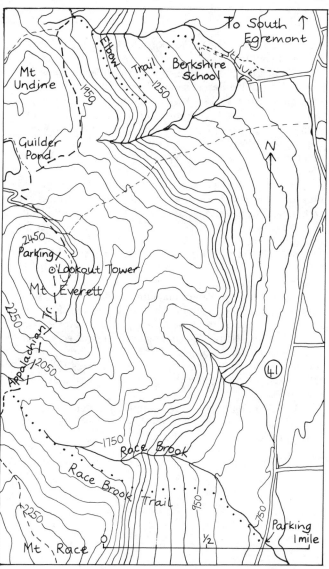

MT. WASHINGTON: MT. EVERETT

the Hudson River. The foundations for the old tower make a picnic site with vistas.

The descent S. from the summit provides the most exciting views of the Berkshire and Litchfield hills, and of the Housatonic River as it snakes into Connecticut. The going is moderately difficult, dropping down steeply over schist with marble outcroppings. The blue-blazed trail, left, where the brook crosses, .7 mi. from the summit (30 min.), takes you through a camping area and down Race Brook Trail to Rte. 41.

You cross a 2-log bridge, under large hemlocks, after 15 min. on Race Brook Trail, as the brook takes form in the wetlands. This interesting process gives you a graphic idea of the meaning of "watershed." At the top of the falls the trail turns left, but you may want to explore this scenic spot. The trail climbs to a lookout (55 min.) with a view into Sheffield. You cross below the upper falls — 5 falls all together descend perhaps 1,300 ft. into the valley.

Rather than the dangerous route beside the falls, a new, 1.5-mi. trail (marked with blue blazes) works its way down the side of the ravine from the upper falls, through the laurel and large hemlocks, coming out at the paved parking area, for a total hiking time of 2.75 hrs. (not counting pausing for the views). Partway down, a side trail leads to middle falls. At the bottom, the trail to lower falls enters from the left.

Turn left on Rte 41. There is ample shoulder to walk on. The school, remember, is on the left, a bit beyond where Berkshire School Rd. enters right.

SHEFFIELD

The southernmost town center in the county is also the generally accepted oldest (1726), no coincidence when you consider that most of the earliest settlers to Berkshire came from Connecticut. Matthew Noble arrived in 1725, alone, from Westfield, however, to make friends with the natives, clear the land, and erect a cabin. Next he fetched his daughter, returning on horseback to set up the first home in Berkshire (then still part of Hampshire County). The first struggles were not with the Indians but with the New York Dutch, who regarded western Berkshire as their own. In 1735, settlers raised the meeting house on Sheffield Plain, a mile north of the present village center.

The first county seat or shire town, when Berkshire became its own county in 1761, Sheffield watched that distinction move gradually north, from Gt. Barrington to Lenox to Pittsfield. Sheffield had its bout with industry, as is true of most Berkshire towns. Marble from quarries in Ashley Falls adorns the custom house in Boston and the court house in New York City. Daniel Shays' Rebellion, a movement of Revolutionary War veterans who felt they had been insufficiently compensated for their services, died in battle with government troops in Sheffield in 1789.

The town exported its sons. Chester Dewey trained for four years at Williams College in the fields (literally) in which he was famous in the first half of the 19th century: botany and geology. Another son, Frederick Augustus Porter Barnard, president of Columbia University, determined that Columbia should include women. Barnard College was named for him shortly after he died in 1889.

WALKS

SALISBURY ROAD

7 miles (2.5 hours)

A most attractive stroll of a serious dimension but generally level, with mixed wooded and open landscape, begins at the junction of Salisbury and Barnum roads. It would make a fine bicycle route. Take Berkshire School Rd. or Root Lane W. from the center of town. Both shortly run into Salisbury Rd., which you should follow left. Park where Barnum, soon to become gravel, enters. Walk along Salisbury to Foley Rd., which bears left. Follow that gravel road to a tangle of roads that cross Schenob Brook. You will pass some lovely real farms and a few gentrified farms, all with distinguished vistas, particularly of Mt. Everett. To make your way through the maze, just keep turning left. You will end up on Barnum St. and, in another 2.0 mi., at your automobile.

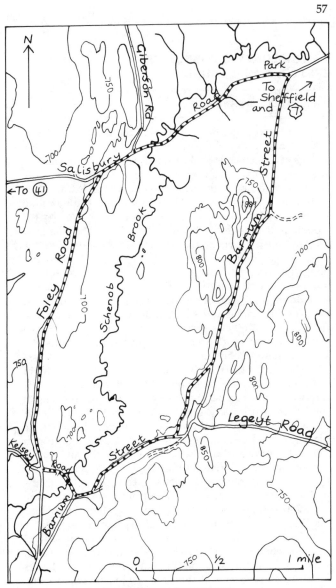

SHEFFIELD: SALISBURY RD.

BARTHOLOMEW'S COBBLE AND
COL. JOHN ASHLEY HOUSE

Various trails available

These two adjacent properties of the Trustees of Reservations are south of the Sheffield town center, near the village of Ashley Falls on the Connecticut line. Turn right on Rte. 7-A, then shortly veer right over railroad tracks onto Rannappo Rd.; continue straight to Cooper Hill Rd. and turn right. The Col. John Ashley House is the oldest still-existing dwelling in Berkshire County, built in 1735. Col. Ashley led troops at the Battle of Bennington (1777). The Sheffield Declaration, written at the Ashley House, preceded the Declaration of Independence by three years. Theodore Sedgwick, originally of Sheffield but later of Stockbridge, successfully defended two of the Ashley slaves, Mum Bett and Brom, who sought freedom under a "born free and equal" clause in the state's constitution. That decision led to the freedom of other slaves in the state. The house is open seasonally for guided tours. A trail from it joins the Bartholomew's Cobble trails.

These can otherwise be reached by continuing straight at Cooper Hill Rd. to Weatogue Rd., just a matter of a few hundred yards, to a parking area on the left. A large map of the Trustees' property shows numerous trails. The ones around the Cobble itself, the rocky eminence between the parking lot and the Housatonic River, are shorter and steeper. These show a remarkable variety of wild flowers and shrubs growing in the rich river bottom land, which is laced with limestone. Bartholomew's Cobble is considered one of the nation's outstanding concentrations of native plants: more than 700 species, including 44 ferns and fern allies. Bird watchers have spotted more than 250 species here.

Trails also range across Weatogue Rd. on open fields and through wooded land. The fields are home to deer and cows, which are sometimes curious but not dangerous. The fences have British-type stiles that enable you to pass where cattle

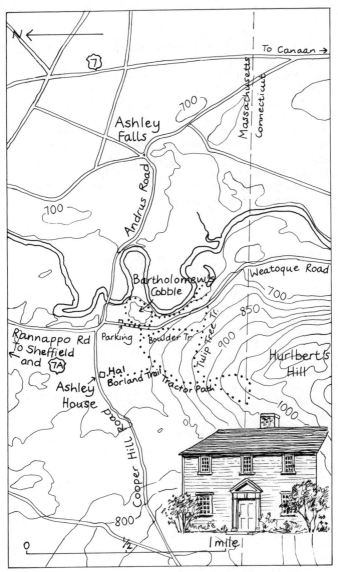

SHEFFIELD: BARTHOLOMEW'S COBBLE & ASHLEY HOUSE

can't. It is possible to stroll about 2 mi., generally following white blazes, up the tractor path to the summit of Hurlbert's Hill, from which there is a lovely view centered on Mt. Everett; then return by the Tulip Tree Trail, which crosses Weatogue Rd. and returns you to the maze of trails by the river. You can cover many of the trails in 2 hours, allowing time to pause for the flora. Try to visit the Cobble in the spring, when the many ephemeral flowers — those that come out before the leaves on the trees shade them — are blossoming, but before the summer traffic hits.

TTOR charges a small fee for a tour of the Ashley house and asks for a donation to tramp the Cobble.

EGREMONT

A township that is two villages (No. and So. Egremont), the Egremonts are gently rolling, even flat, compared to upland neighboring Mt. Washington. But the walking is great here, offering extraordinarily long views for those who have neither the time nor the inclination to scale a peak. Back in the early history of Egremont, one man who wanted to remain on the plain was Gen. Henry Knox, who entered Berkshire through the Egremonts in 1776, with soldiers, 124 yoke of oxen, and 58 captured cannon from Ft. Ticonderoga — all en route to Boston to help George Washington drive out the British. These days you'll find a few good shops (including a sporting goods store, open fall and winter only) and three noteworthy restaurants in So. Egremont, and one fine restaurant and a classic country general store in No. Egremont. That's it.

WALK

BALDWIN HILL ROAD NORTH AND SOUTH

6.0 miles or less (2.5 hours, round trip)

Start from either So. or No. Egremont, or station a car in each village. If you begin this round trip at the general store in No. Egremont, corner of Rte. 71 and No. Egremont-Hillsdale Rd. (at sign for Prospect Lake), go W. through a residential area for .1 mi. and turn left onto Baldwin Hill Rd. N & S (gravel), which rises gently for .6 mi. while passing by French Park on the right and through woods. The road flattens out as you begin to leave the woods; vistas appear in all directions. Pass pungent Bel Air Farm on the right and admire the vast cornfields. At 1.1 mi. (25 min.), cross the intersection of Baldwin Hill Rd. E & W. Your view includes: to the west, Catamount Ski Area; to the southwest, Mt. Everett; to the south, the Litchfield Hills in Connecticut; to the east, Monument Mtn. and Warner Mtn. (the latter to the east of Gt. Barrington, which is hidden from view, down in a valley).

The road slopes gently downwards now toward So. Egremont. Note the airplanes rising and descending near the Gt. Barrington Airport in the valley to the east. At 2.0 mi. (50 min.), cross the intersection with Town House Hill Rd. At 2.2 mi., pass a small (private) pond left. The road is now paved and rising slightly. By 2.6 mi. it's all downhill into So. Egremont, where at Rte. 23 (3.0 mi.; 1:15 min.) you turn left and go 100 yds. to the deli or restaurant for a snack before heading back.

Alternatives include: side trips on Baldwin Hill Rd. E & W. Either way is good, although neither has any destination of note. Going E., you'll probably want to descend to just past a large white farmhouse in the pines right, then turn around and retrace your steps. Total mileage without the sidetrip is 6.0 (2.5 hrs.); with the sidetrip, 6.8.

NEW MARLBOROUGH

Benjamin Wheeler came from Marlborough, Massachusetts, in 1736, because his home town had been granted this western territory. He would have starved the first winter if some folks from Sheffield hadn't heard of his plight and struggled through the snow to his relief. But he had sufficient spirit to stick it out and invite the rest of his family to join him the next summer.

The town now has a population of 1,021, pretty well spread out. The town center is on Rte. 57, which drops south from Rte. 23 east of Gt. Barrington. Other village centers in New Marlborough township are: Hartsville, near beautiful Lake Buel, Mill River and Konkapot on the Konkapot River, Southfield, at the junction of New Marlborough and East Hill roads, Gomorrah and Clayton in the south. The town has more defined villages than any other in the county. The road signs are so thorough and numerous they virtually require you to stop the car to read them, which may be just what the citizens of New Marlborough want.

WALKS

HARMON ROAD

New Marlborough and Monterey, 7 miles (2.5 hours)

A stroll begins at New Marlborough village and follows New Marlborough-Monterey Rd. (bear right at the fork) into Monterey, past the Trout Pond on Harmon Brook. You are still on the road when you turn left. Turn left again on Harmon Rd., back to the point of origin. This is a fine bike route. Rawson Brook Farm at the Monterey end sells goat cheese. the Old Inn on the Green, at the Marlborough end, is a lovely spot for a cool drink.

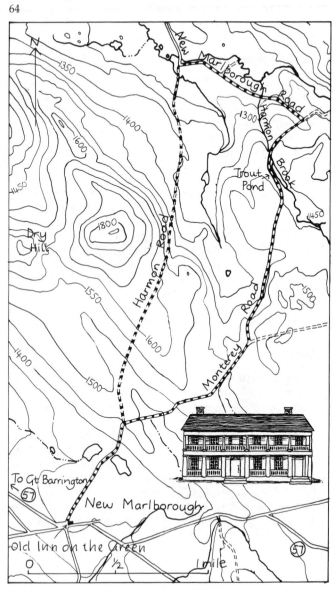

NEW MARLBOROUGH: HARMON RD.

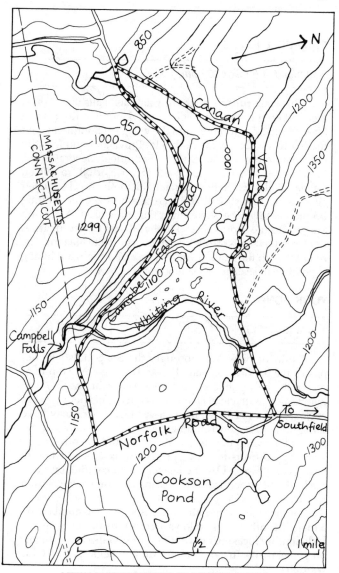

NEW MARLBOROUGH: CAMPBELL FALLS

CAMPBELL FALLS

Southfield, 4.5 miles (2 hours)

This walk runs through the Campbell Falls State Forest area just on the state line. Follow the Southfield Rd. S. from New Marlborough center into the village of Southfield, and the Norfolk Rd. S. from Southfield. Provisions and friendly information are available at the Southfield General Store. Park near Cookson Pond. Walk N. on Norfolk to left on Canaan Valley Rd., left on Canaan Rd. (both gravel), and left again on Campbell Falls Rd. across a bridge over Whiting Brook that might be wetter than the brook itself. A parking area marks the short side trip to the falls (in Connecticut). A final, brief left on Norfolk Rd. should complete the tour. The road through the state forest may be a bit rough, but biking is possible in season and skiing in the winter.

YORK POND

1 mile (30 min.)

South of New Marlborough, the So. Sandisfield Rd. passes the Sandisfield State Forest. Don't go by. Stop in at one of the best public swimming areas in the county, well maintained, with clean changing rooms. (This popular area is closed when 300 swimmers assemble, so you may have difficulty parking on a summer weekend.) Gasoline engines aren't allowed on the lake, so it is clean and inviting once it warms up. Efforts to keep open the walk around the lake have been thwarted by the beavers, who continually flood the trail. The supervisor is preparing 2 half-mile walks from HQ. One will lead to a former CCC camp and be self-guided, with numbers on foundations corresponding to numbers on a map. The other walk follows a gravel road to the grave of Josh Smith, a local resident. Other lovely walks are available on gravel roads. Just down the road is a memorial to 5 CCC wardens.

GREAT BARRINGTON

Gt. Barrington became the focus for southern Berkshire — the shopping center for the hilltowns that surround it, home to a registry of deeds, a court, and other status symbols. Nowadays it boasts fine restaurants, theaters, bookstores, a college, and numerous other amenities. Along with the center of town, on Rte. 7, there is an old mill area at Housatonic, still home to Rising Paper Co. Originally settled in 1726 at the Great Fordway on the Housatonic, which gave way to the Great Bridge, the town is also on the old Great Rd. from Boston to Albany (roughly Rte. 23 now), so it is no wonder that although named after Viscount Barrington, it magnified the name. By tradition, the Indian village that preceded the town was named Mahaiwe, or "place down stream." A venerable theater in town retains the name.

Back in the days when Americans and British were on the same side, Gen. Jeffrey Amherst, on his way to Ticonderoga, camped with his troops where the Great Rd. crossed the Green River. The town, after separating from Sheffield in 1761, became a seat of discontent with British rule. In August, 1774, a group of men seized the court house, preventing the King's Court from holding session. Thus the town claims the "first open resistance to British rule in America." Yet the town's residents included many Tories — notably leading citizen David Ingersoll, who was imprisoned in Litchfield, Connecticut, and then exiled. British General Johnny Burgoyne, marching in defeat from Saratoga on the Great Rd. during the Revolutionary War, was feted in Gt. Barrington; during Shays' uprising of dissident veterans the court house was once again seized.

William Cullen Bryant, this country's first native-born poet, practiced law in Gt. Barrington. A poem of his told of an unhappy Indian love affair culminating with her leap from Squaw Peak on Monument Mtn., north of the center of town. A more vivid attempt to explain the cairn or stone pile by the trail records that when the Indian maiden was hurled from the summit, she caught hold of a branch on the way down and remained suspended for two days, howling all the while, until a lightning bolt struck the tree, dropping both maiden and branch to oblivion. Her Mahican Indian relatives built the cairn in her memory, to which passers-by continue to add stones.

In a different application of electricity, William Stanley tested his theory of alternating current by providing street lighting for his home town, the first commercial use of electric current. The Housatonic Agricultural Society and its successors have held a fair at the Barrington Fairgrounds in summers ever since 1842.

Camping
The nearest campground is at Benedict Pond, Beartown State Forest, E. on Rte. 23 to forest HQ. Follow the signs along Blue Hill Rd. from there. The parking fee is modest. Lifeguards protect the swimming beach in season. At Monument Mtn., Rte. 7 N. of town, the picnic grove (910 ft. in elevation) is a lovely, shaded spot.

WALKS

SEEKONK

Gt. Barrington and Alford, 3 or 6 miles (1 or 2 hours)

Road approach

Either 2 short or 1 long hike can be enjoyed on the east side of town and into Alford. Drive up Taconic St. at St. James Church, which becomes Alford Rd. after curving right. Follow Alford Rd. down hill past Simon's Rock College and then, soon, bear left on Seekonk Rd. where the walk begins.

SEEKONK

Park carefully by the small bridge. Most of these roads are gravel. Walk S. on Round Hill Rd., looking out from high farms. Turn right on Seekonk Cross Rd. and then either right on Seekonk back to the beginning or left on Green River Rd., right on No. Egremont Rd., right on Cross Rd., and right again on Seekonk Cross Rd. Left on Seekonk to the beginning. (The brook in these parts is known alternately as Alford or Seekonk.) This is a fine rolling stroll or bicycle ride with lovely panoramic views.

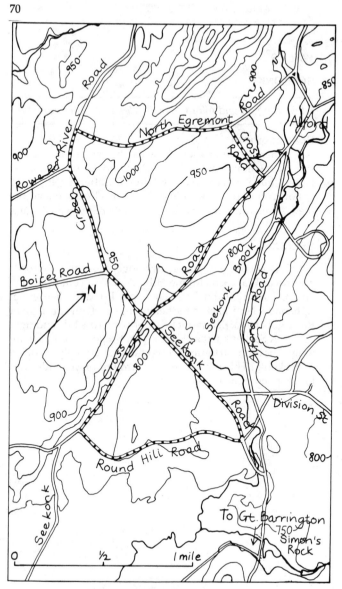

GREAT BARRINGTON: SEEKONK

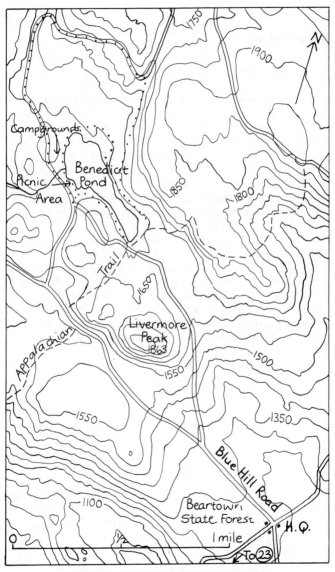

GREAT BARRINGTON: BENEDICT POND

BENEDICT POND

1.5 miles (40 mins.) for shorter loop

Another walk can be reached from Gt. Barrington's Monument Valley Rd. Coming S. on Rte. 7, turn left just beyond the high school. Turn left on Stony Brook Rd., which becomes Blue Hill Rd. A bicycling expedition from Monument Valley Rd. is 12 mi. Turn left into Benedict Pond to walk a longer or shorter circuit. There is a small parking fee in season. Bikers will want to do a 3.5 mi. road trip around Benedict Pond. Walkers can circumambulate on a 1.5 mi. trail, blazed blue. This fine swimming area, presided over by lifeguards, is available, together with the changing rooms and outhouses. The pond is lovely; the woods and cliffs behind, dramatic.

The AT passes through Beartown State Forest, with a shelter S. of Mt. Wilcox, which the AT does not climb. That peak rises 2,112 ft., without much of a view because the lookout tower is closed. It is a relatively easy climb (4.0 mi. round trip) from the pond. Beartown is busy in the winter with snowmobiles and cross-country skiers.

HIKE

MONUMENT MOUNTAIN

3.0 miles (1.5 hours)

Road approaches

Monument Mtn. is a pillar of stones, unmistakable to the motorist on Rte. 7, located just north of the center of the town of Gt. Barrington, a few mi. south of Stockbridge and slightly south of Monument Mtn. Regional High School. Of the several parking lots on the west side of the road, the one at the picnic grounds (with the green Trustees of Reservations sign) is handiest for the hike described here.

MONUMENT MOUNTAIN

TTOR maintains this 503-acre reservation (and asks you to make a contribution if you hike it). This pile of stones has a largely clear ridge, giving you a good look at Beartown State Forest to the east, the Taconic Range to the west and the valleys in between. If it isn't a tradition at the regional high school below the mountain for seniors to hike to the summit, it ought to be. This is less of a wilderness hike than others in this guide. From the summit, as well as the panorama of unspoiled land, you can look directly into a former landfill operation and onto the whizzing vehicles of Rte. 7 — it depends where you choose to look.

Although not lengthy, this is a steep, rugged climb. Also a storied one. In 1850, a publisher arranged an outing for several writers on this mountain: Herman Melville, Nathaniel Hawthorne, and Oliver Wendell Holmes. The account of the wagon loaded with picnic goods, including champagne, and the liveried servants who accompanied them, may make you question how they made it up the trail. You will find out.

The well-trod trail, which is blazed white, leaves from the north corner of the parking lot, near a large map. It is moderately steep, passing through hemlocks, with scree (rocky rubble at the bottom of a slope) on the left. A trail enters right in 5 min. In a quarter hr., faced with a ravine, you swing left. Ignore all other trails, many of which are detours, keeping to the left. The stream on the right flows in lovely waterfalls in the spring. In places the trail is badly eroded, although the Trustees have labored hard at stone water bars, to try to deflect the freshets.

Turn left again at 22 min., on the trail to Squaw Peak. Almost immediately you pass a rock with the year the (then-called) Trustees of Public Reservations acquired the first portion of the property: 1899. The trail is quite steep, soon requiring clambering over quartzite boulders. The look-out left seems to be directly over the school. You are on the summit ridge in half an hour, but persevere, through the pitch pine, to the peak that honors an Indian maid, thought, at least by the poet, to have flung herself to her death. Pay attention to your footing, which is rough. The rocks themselves, with their lichens, are intriguing. One impending rock has the date 1888 carved in it, albeit painted over by more recent visitors.

To leave, follow back the way you came for 5 min. Then turn left just beyond the inscribed boulder. Note you are on more of a road; indeed the old carriage road up which the literary party came. Suddenly you sense something has changed. Consider. You hear more birds, not necessarily because they are louder but because you have rounded a corner of the cobble, leaving the state highway traffic noises behind you. Again, keep left as various trails enter. The going is much more gradual than on the way up. The hemlocks are larger. Even bigger are the boulders that have tumbled down the steep sides in this romantic spot.

Gradually you begin to hear the road sounds again, as you work around the south end of the mountain. A relatively newly cut trail takes you parallel with Rte. 7, N. to the picnic ground, which you reach after 1:17 walking time — not counting the time you lingered at the summit.

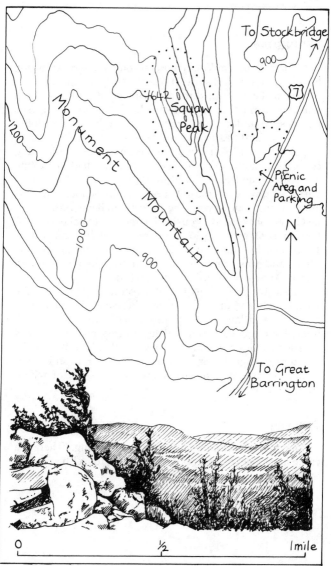

To Stockbridge

900

7

1200

Monument Mountain

1642 Squaw Peak

1000

900

Picnic Area and Parking

N

To Great Barrington

0   ½   1 mile

GREAT BARRINGTON: MONUMENT MTN.

TYRINGHAM

The Tyringham Valley remains one of the most lovely, bucolic views in Berkshire. It has stayed that way honestly. No railroad ever came through town, no interurban trolleys nor even a numbered highway. Like Williamstown, it is nearly surrounded by mountains, nestled between October Mtn.   and Beartown state forests.

Settled in 1735, Tyringham has always been a farming community, although over the years it has had just a bite of many of the treats served up more extensively in other Berkshire towns. It is the only town in Massachusetts named after a woman, however: Jane Tyringham Beresford, Colonial Governor Bernard's cousin. A handful of Shakers settled here in 1792, growing to a community of 100, cultivating 1,500 acres by mid-19th century when they began to fade. Their land was purchased to build an elaborate summer colony, known as Fernside, on Hop Brook.

Industry arrived in the 19th century, especially the Steadman Rake Company. Richard Watson Gilder, editor of *Scribner's* and later *Century* magazines, arrived in 1898 to build Four Brooks Farm, which attracted the literary and artistic notables of the day, from naturalist John Burroughs to sculptor Augustus Saint-Gaudens to historian and writer Henry Adams to humorist Mark Twain — all of whom summered here.

Camping

Tyringham remains free of tourist trappings. There is a campsite, however, at Upper Goose Pond, for AT hikers, just over the line from Tyringham in Lee.

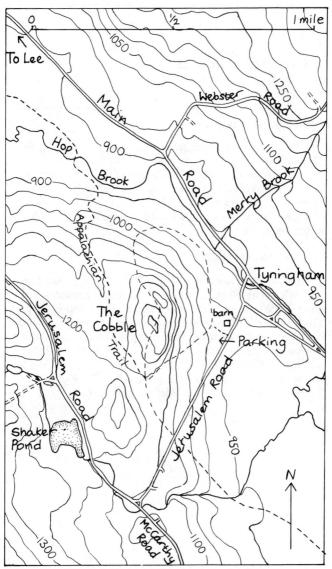

TYRINGHAM: TYRINGHAM COBBLE

WALK

THE TYRINGHAM COBBLE

2 miles (1 hour)

Road approaches

To get to Tyringham from the Lee interchange of the Massachusetts Turnpike, at the junction of Rte. 20 jog briefly right on Rte. 102 W., then take Tyringham Rd. due S. Turn right at the town center on Jerusalem Rd. Stay right where Church St. enters. Soon you will see a TTOR sign, right, just beyond a real barn. Park in the lot. Note information in kiosk and follow trail along fence.

THE TYRINGHAM COBBLE

Follow blue blazes into the woods. To make the loop clockwise, bear left at main trail, which briefly coincides with the AT. The trail enters a wooded area and then comes out on a rocky outlook, the obvious picnic site. The white church and country town are picturesquely set against the wooded hillsides surrounding Goose Pond. The trail descends, through additional stiles, parallels the town's main street, and gradually swings right back to the trail junction. TTOR owns 206 acres, to which the trail provides an introduction.

STOCKBRIDGE

This 250-year-old town (incorporated in 1739) started out chartered by England's King George II to "the Housatannack Tribe of Indians . . . to their use and behoof forever." The Europeans who settled there had a notion they could improve the lot of the Indians, however, which led eventually — as it often did — to the Indians being driven out.

The one-armed Rev. John Sergeant, who took the trouble to learn the Mahican language, arrived as first missionary in 1734, teaching Chiefs Konkapot and Umpachene domestic skills like agriculture and house building. His true friendship attracted Indians from many miles away. Jonathan Edwards succeeded him. While well disposed to the Native Americans, he was preoccupied with his religious writings and hectored by those Christian families sent to be worthy examples to the Indians, such as that of Ephraim Williams, Sr. This worthy sold them liquor and connived to acquire their land. So the Indian village became the center of the European town. In 1783 the natives held their last campfire here and migrated to a reservation in western New York State and thence to Wisconsin.

When Judge Theodore Sedgwick moved to Stockbridge from Sheffield in 1785, he stamped the place an important and wealthy town. By the 1860s, like Lenox, it had become the country seat for many influential eastern families. It attracted artists, like Daniel Chester French, who designed the seated Lincoln in the Lincoln Memorial, and Norman Rockwell, the magazine illustrator. It planned well, creating the Laurel Hill Association in 1835, the first village improvement organization in this country, and saving its most precious buildings and historic sites. The Laurel Hill Assoc. is still active, meeting annually, its members planting trees and maintaining trails.

Several of the early and staunch (European) families: the Sergeants, Woodbridges, Williamses, Dwights, Stoddards, Edwardses, Sedgwicks, Fields, Butlers, Choates, Parsonses, Rathbuns, Guerrieris, Burghardts, still have scions in town or nearby. Seven U.S. ambassadors have lived here: Cyrus

Field, who laid the Atlantic cable, and his equally remarkable brothers; three men educated here sat on the U.S. Supreme Court at the same time: Henry Billings Brown, Stephen J. Field, and David Joshua Brewer. Its recent residents also include the famous and respected, such as psychoanalyst Erik Erikson and theologian Reinhold Neibuhr. And of course one day in the 1960s, according to the song, Officer Obie arrested Arlo Guthrie for throwing some trash from Alice's Restaurant by a Stockbridge roadside.

The town center, which looks like . . . well, a Norman Rockwell *Saturday Evening Post* cover, is the most choked by summer tourists of any Berkshire town. People park a mile out along all the highways to visit the Indian Mission House (the actual building, although not in its original location), Naumkeag (the Choate mansion, now, like the Mission House, under the care of TTOR), the many upscale shops and, at the center of things, the Red Lion Inn. A bit farther out, you will find Berkshire Theatre Festival, Chesterwood (the sculptor's home), Berkshire Botanical Garden and, at the north end of town, the Norman Rockwell Museum, the Stockbridge Bowl, and Tanglewood (summer home of the Boston Symphony Orchestra).

WALKS

ICE GLEN

3.5 miles or shorter (1.5 hours)

Strolls in Stockbridge are legion and lovely, not to mention the fact that summer and early fall biking or even walking is speedier than automobiling. The Laurel Hill Assoc. publishes a *Hike and Bike Guide*, available at town hall or library, with a useful set of maps.

Start with the Ice Glen, maintained by the Laurel Hill Assoc. Beginning at the Red Lion Inn, walk S. half a mi. on Rte. 7 to Ice Glen Rd., beyond the bridge. Follow this small lane for .5 mi. Turn left. Follow the signs in what looks like a private drive to the trail. (It is possible to leave a car at Rte. 7 and start from the other side.) The yellow-blazed trail, although short, is rough, in spite of noble efforts to ease the way over boulders and around large, prone hemlocks. It gets its name from the fact that ice lasts longer in the stony crevasse than anywhere else around. Every other Halloween the town stages a scary parade through the glen, a tradition going back 100 years.

After climbing 100 feet through the tangled glen and reading the carving in the cliff crediting David Dudley Field, Jr. for donating the property to the town, you can turn right to ascend another 465 feet in elevation to Laura's Tower. The steel tower at the top, on a clear day, gives a fine view of the Berkshire Hills from Mt. Everett and Race Mtn. to Mt. Greylock, not to mention downtown Stockbridge. Descend from the tower as you came up, but turn right on the main trail across the Memorial Footbridge, and back to town by Park and South streets. Total mileage, starting at the Red Lion and including Laura's Tower: 3.5 mi.

To avoid the rough section through the glen and shorten the trip, start on the Memorial Footbridge side, climb to the tower, and return. You can find a trail behind the Plain School or walk out Park St.

BOWKER'S WOODS

.5 mile (15 minutes)

A short trail passes near the loop in the Housatonic and across the freight line and old interurban trolley right-of-way to give you a look at Bowker's Woods. To get there, go W. on Main St. from the Red Lion Inn, continue straight at the Chime Tower, past the Indian Burial Ground on a knoll to the left, cross the river and bear right up the hill and out Glendale Rd. to a discrete opening in the stone wall, right, for the Lower Trail (1.5 mi. from the inn, not included in mileage). This is an easy and pleasant stroll, passing along a bluff by the river with lovely views. To get to the Upper Trail, which winds through some lovely pines, bear right twice after cross-ing the river, following Glendale North Rd. to Rte. 183. Jog right and left, just beyond a small pond, for the entrance to the trail.

PROSPECT HILL

3 miles (1 hour)

A fine route for stroll or bike takes you up Prospect Hill and back on Church St. Begin directly across Main St. from the Red Lion Inn, on Pine St. Pass the tennis courts, then bear left on Prospect Hill Rd. and continue up to Naumkeag, the James H. Choate home designed in 1885 by Sanford White. Swing left on Old Meetinghouse Hill Rd., beyond, and thence by Field St. (gravel) back to Church St., getting a look at the attractive backside of Naumkeag on your way to the Chime Tower, where you turn left for the inn.

The Marian Fathers, across the road from Naumkeag, allow walkers on their extensive grounds, for an alternative route, or you can extend the trip by a mile by continuing up Prospect Hill to Larrywaug Rd. and then down N. Church St.

GLENDALE

Several alternatives

Another set of walks and bike rides lies to the west and a bit south of Stockbridge in the village of Glendale. From the Red Lion Inn in Stockbridge follow Main St. W. by the Town Hall, Chime Tower, and the Indian Burial Ground and across the river to Glendale Rd., past the entrance to Bowker's Woods Lower Trail and S. on Castle Hill Rd. Turn left on Cherry Hill Rd. and left again on Cherry St. to the beginning (3.0 mi.). And/or venture farther out Glendale Rd., by auto perhaps, across the railroad tracks and over the river a second time to Rte. 183. Park at the Glendale Post Office and walk straight ahead up a short, steep section of Christian Hill Rd. to gravel Williamsville Rd. Turn left. Soon on your right is Chesterwood, once the home of sculptor Daniel Chester French and now a National Trust museum. Bear right at the fork to Dugway Rd., also gravel. Turn left there, along Mohawk Lake Brook to Rte. 183 and along the river, past the restored hydroelectric plant, and back to the point of origin. Although Rte. 183 winds charmingly along the Housatonic, vehicles travel too fast. Use caution or avoid Rte. 183 by retracing your footsteps.

GOULD MEADOWS AND BULLARD WOODS

Various options

Neither of these lovely properties has a trail system but both are open to the public for wandering. Both are off Hawthorne Rd., paralleling the northern side of Stockbridge Bowl (note: Hawthorne *St.*, confusingly, is perpendicular to Hawthorne *Rd.* and heads toward Lenox). There is a map at the Gould Meadows parking area, a few hundred yards down Rte. 183 from Hawthorne Rd. (you are near Tanglewood, to N., and near the site, to S., of the canoe portion of the Great Josh Billings Runaground, held annually in the fall). The higher land provides a remarkable view of the Bowl and excellent picnicking. Carry out any trash, please. You can wander down to the water if you like.

Bullard Woods is cited by state foresters as the best place in the county to see large trees. A scruffy field at the corner of Hawthorne St. and Rd. provides parking; if you look carefully you will see a sign at the edge of the field. Logging roads curve through the 50-acre stand of enormous oaks, especially along the edge of the meadow. Other large trees include sugar maples; shag bark hickory; large tulip poplar, including one about 4 feet in circumference, with a faded sign attached; and many large white pines — including one 18 feet in circumference, barred from being a record because it appears to have been formed when two trees grew together. Stumps in the woods show where chestnuts were cut in response to the blight (pre-1920).

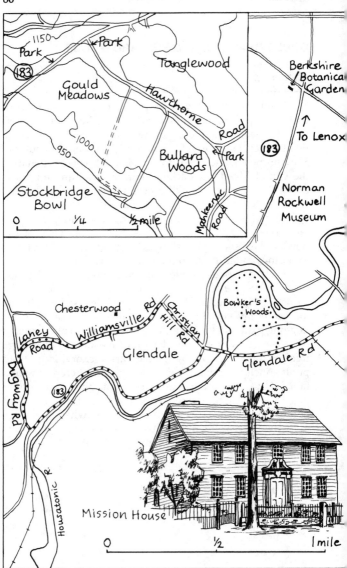

1150
Park
Park
Tanglewood
(183)
Gould
Meadows
Hawthorne
Road
Berkshire
Botanical
Garden
↑
To Lenox
(183)
1000
Bullard
Woods
Park
950
Stockbridge
Bowl
Norman
Rockwell
Museum
0   ¼   ½ mile
Makheenac Road

Chesterwood
Williamsville Rd
Christian Hill Rd
Bowker's
Woods
Lahey
Road
Williamsville Road
Glendale
Glendale Rd
Dugway Rd
(183)
Housatonic R.
Mission House
0   ½   1 mile

STOCKBRIDGE: WALKS

STOCKBRIDGE: WALKS

CENTRAL COUNTY

LENOX

Lenox is not at all what you see from Rte. 7, a strip of shops and restaurants. The old center of town is on Rte. 7-A; that, too, has a touristy inclination but is recognizable as a community with a rich history.

Originally connected to the outside world only by an Indian path that followed the Housatonic River, Yokun-town was first settled in 1750 and named after Chief Yokun, a Stockbridge Indian. When the town was incorporated, in 1767, it was named for Charles Lennox, Duke of Richmond. At some time, one *n* was deemed sufficient; the opposite of the inclination that added "great" to Viscount Barrington's name. Considered a home to Tories during the Revolutionary War, by early in the 19th century Lenox boasted thriving industries that led it to replace Gt. Barrington as the shire town: hence the court house (1816), now the Lenox Library. Pittsfield usurped the county seat in 1868.

Lenox changed utterly, however, when Charles Sedgwick moved there in 1821. Shortly thereafter, his sister, writer Catherine Sedgwick, joined him. Together they hosted the literary lights of the day and inspired other families to build great estates in town, the so-called cottages designed on the Newport, Rhode Island, model. Many well-to-do gentry from New York and Boston developed large estates in and around Lenox, tastefully tucking their enormous homes out of sight behind shrubbery. Few of these remain in private hands now. The most famous visitor at the time was the British actress Fanny Kemble, who charmed the community and to whom Longfellow addressed a sonnet. She donated the proceeds of a reading to pay for the clock in the tower of Lenox's lovely Church on the Hill.

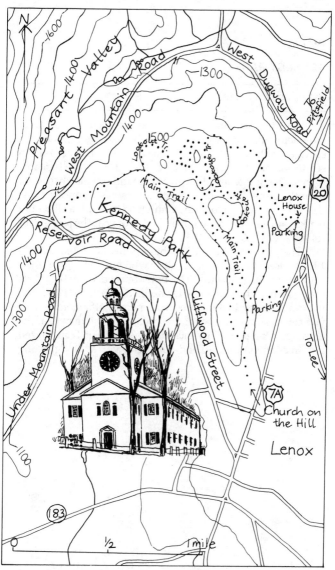

LENOX: KENNEDY PARK

WALKS

KENNEDY PARK

3-4 miles (1.5 hours)

A history of large estates — as opposed to farm land, cut-over land, or developed land — has left some of the largest trees in the county in Lenox and Stockbridge, as you can see in Bullard Woods or driving through these fashionable towns. One gorgeous glimpse of the kind of land that is not recently grown-over farm fields is Lenox's Kennedy Park. Best access is just beyond the Church on the Hill, well within walking distance of downtown, or the lot near the junction of routes 7 and 7-A.

The area was the site of the Aspinwall Hotel, built in 1902 to accommodate the wealthy who wanted to visit their cottage-dwelling friends. The hotel burned in 1931 and its grounds became the John D. Kennedy Park in 1957. The main trail, blazed white, breeds numerous offshoots, so that you can design your own route, consulting the map near the entrance. One possibility includes the Lookout Trail, blazed red. In combination, red and white give you an invigorating stroll.

RESERVOIRS

Lenox and Richmond, 8 miles or less (3 hours or less)

A pleasant and lengthy walk begins outside Pleasant Valley, the Audubon wildlife sanctuary on West Mountain Rd., heading west. West Mountain Rd. becomes Reservoir Rd., passing Upper Root Reservoir (right) and then quite small Large Reservoir (left). At the fork, follow Reservoir Rd. right and then left. You are in the town of Richmond now, once a part of Yokuntown but split off when the Bay Colony sold the tracts of "Indian Land." Keep straight where Lenox Rd. enters right and bear left with it around Fairfield Pond (about 4 mi.). The next left turn will return you to Large Reservoir, whence you can follow Reservoir and West roads back to your point of departure. Some remarkable homes jut out of swiftly falling hillsides. En route you will see also wooded and pasture land. Variations are available, by taking different turns. A good bicycle route, with even more variations than for hiking, depending on ambition.

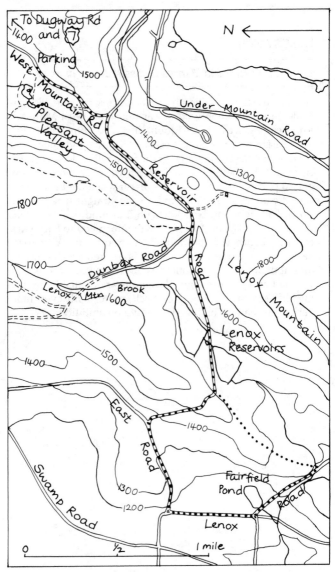

To Dugway Rd and Parking

1400

1500

N ←

West Mountain Rd

Pleasant Valley

1800

1700

Dunbar Road

Lenox Mtn Brook 1600

1400

1500

Under Mountain Road

1400

1500

Reservoir

1300

Road

Lenox Mountain

1800

1600

Lenox Reservoirs

East Road

1300

1200

Swamp Road

1400

Fairfield Pond

Road

Lenox

0   ½   1 mile

LENOX: RESERVOIRS

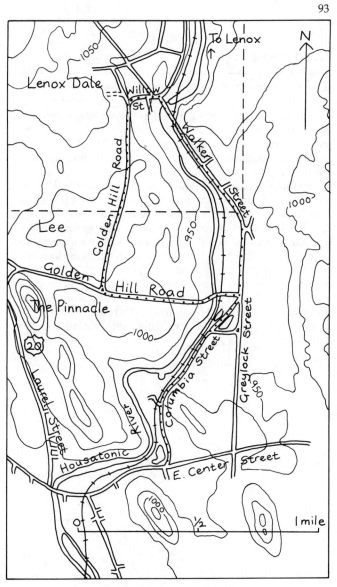

LEE/LENOX: GOLDEN HILL

GOLDEN HILL

Lee, Lenoxdale, and Lenox, 2.5 miles (1 hour)

Stride along Golden Hill Rd. in Lenox, where striking agricultural fields set in the Berkshire Hills gradually become residential. To get there follow Rte. 20 (from the north) to the built-up center of Lee and turn left onto Columbia St., driving until you find a good parking place. Then follow Columbia, Greylock, and Walker streets to Willow Hill Rd. in Lenoxdale. Turn left on Willow St., at right angle up the hill (off Walker St., which continues on a diagonal) until you meet Golden Hill Rd. (which is T-shaped). Left again, on the highlands, looking into the Housatonic Valley and across it . . . behold October Mtn. State Forest. Turn left again, looking at the same view over fields of Queen Anne's lace and loosestrife. The route extends down the hill, across the narrow bridge over the river and back to the tracks, your shining path to your car, less than 2.5 mi. total. The route, without the portion on the tracks, is available, with variations, for bicycling.

HIKE

PLEASANT VALLEY / LENOX MOUNTAIN

3 miles (1.5 hours)

Road approaches

Pleasant Valley Wildlife Sanctuary is off the Lenox-Pittsfield Rd. (Rtes. 7 & 20). Turn west on W. Dugway Rd., at the sanctuary sign, N. of the junction with Rte. 7-A but S. of the junction of Holmes Rd. Follow Dugway, a black-topped road, a mile until it ends at W. Mountain Rd. Bear left on this gravel road for .8 mi. The sanctuary has parking lots on both sides of the road. It is closed on Mondays.

Restrooms are available in the barn. Maps and other interesting pamphlets are available at the window, where non-members of Massachusetts Audubon will be asked to pay a small fee for use of the sanctuary. There are no shelters or camping areas on this hike. Incidentally, no dogs are allowed on this property. Collecting of plants, of course, is not allowed; nor is it on any public lands or most private lands.

The Pleasant Valley Wildlife Sanctuary, one of three Massachusetts Audubon properties in the county, was established in 1929. Seven miles of trails wind through 1,100 acres of Berkshire uplands and beaver swamps. A trailside museum is open mid-May through October.

PLEASANT VALLEY / LENOX MOUNTAIN

This is a lovely short hike, relatively steep, with a rewarding view from the summit of Lenox Mtn. Other strategic lookouts along the trail survey the surroundings. At least in the spring, trails follow delightful brooks with sparkling waterfalls.

From the Audubon administration building follow the main trail, past the barn on the left and the Trailside Museum on the right. From this spot you can see the destination: the tower on the ridge to the west. (Audubon plans new buildings, which will change the configuration.) The Bluebird Trail passes through fields that are beginning to fill in with second growth. Audubon is displaying the way first weeds replace grass, bushes replace weeds, and gradually trees fill in former farm land. In this area, pines come to shield out undergrowth, and then, finally, hardwoods take over from the pines.

Follow straight ahead as two trails depart to the right. At the sanctuary all trails heading away from the administration building are blazed blue; all returning to the center are blazed yellow. Cross trails are blazed white. It is difficult to get lost.

At the bottom of the slope, cross a bridge over Yokun Brook under a stand of tall pines, leave a beaver swamp on the right, and cross a second bridge (at 8 min.), following signs to the tower at various intersections. The trail continues up the brook you just crossed. (You may want to detour on alternate trails to examine the industrious beavers' activities.)

At the 4-way intersection (12 min.), go straight. The brook is on the left. As you gain elevation, laurel, which blossoms in June, begins to fill in under hardwood trees. You pass out of the sanctuary land into Lenox watershed lands, but Audubon maintains trails throughout. The trail weaves back and forth across the brook, which runs in the spring with several falls. Large hemlocks aim to the sky in the ravines and along the ledges. The schist over which the water runs contains quartz outcroppings. At 30 min. the trail begins to skirt a ledge, left. In 40 min. you come out on the summit.

The view from the summit looks down onto Richmond Pond, which seems to be very close, in spite of the 2,126 ft. of elevation. (You have climbed 786 ft. from the office.) The Catskill Mtns. rise in the southwest. The Taconic highlands to the northwest are in Pittsfield State Forest. Lake Onota lies to the west northwest. Looking east you see the highlands of October Mtn. State Forest. To the southeast you look down into the extremely pleasant valley. The tower adds some 80 ft. of *up* to the view.

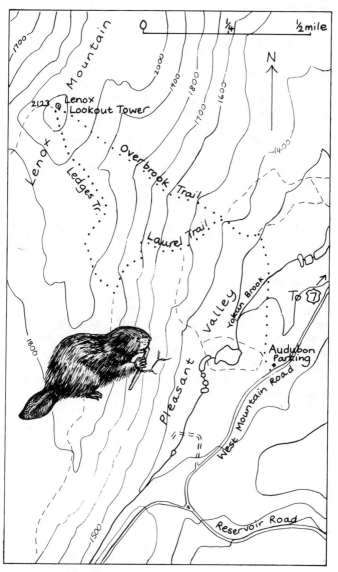

1700

½ mile
¼
0

N

Mountain

2000
1900
1800
1600

1700
1400

2123 ○ Lenox
Lookout Tower

Lenox

Overbrook Trail

Ledges Tr.

Laurel Trail

Pleasant Valley

Yokun Brook

To 7

Audubon
Parking

1800

West Mountain Road

1500

Reservoir Road

LENOX: PLEASANT VALLEY / LENOX MTN.

Follow the Ledges Trail to the SE rather than the jeep road. Remember, returning trails are blazed yellow. In 4 min. you begin to pass over more ledges, descending and climbing along the ridge. At 1:02 from the administration building you come to a trail junction at Fairview, which gives another nice look into the sanctuary's 670 acres. Turn left on the aptly named Laurel Trail, which begins a steep descent part of which is in a stream bed. The hardwoods now include oak, birch, and beech.

At 1:15 go straight at the intersection with the Ravine Trail. At 1:19, bear right at a familiar 4 corners. You are now back on the trail you began climbing, appropriately known as Overbrook. Although you have been traversing rocky outcroppings, the valley lies atop limestone, buffering the effects of acid rain and affording hospitable conditions for certain ferns and other rare species. Bear right at the Y. At 1:24 cross the first bridge and at 1:30 min., pass the administration building.

The sanctuary map shows numerous other strolls and hikes, the one to the tower being the most rigorous. You could spend a full day walking through this beautifully maintained property and enjoying a picnic. Massachusetts Audubon organizes many educational activities, including cross-country skiing and snowshoeing on this property and at Canoe Meadows, another Berkshire sanctuary, located a few miles N., off Holmes Rd. in Pittsfield.

RICHMOND

So near and yet so far. While a noisy Sunday afternoon Tanglewood traffic jam has clogged the roads through neighboring Lenox and nearby Stockbridge, just over the mountain is silent and almost forgotten Richmond, enjoying its emptiness. This is a town without a center, but it does have fine roads to walk. Here's one.

WALK

EAST ROAD

4.6 miles or less (2 hours)

Road approaches

From W. Stockbridge take Pittsfield Rd., which shortly becomes Swamp Rd., heading N. (at start in the village, be careful not to confuse Pittsfield/Swamp roads with Rte. 41). Go a little over 2 mi. to the Lenox Rd. where you turn right and then park after driving in 100 yds. or so. Park carefully: there is no official lot. East Rd. departs obliquely to left, rising.

From Tanglewood: Pass the Main Gate on Rte. 183, going S., and veer right, up the Richmond Mtn. Rd., passing Apple Tree Inn right. After climbing through several twisty turns, ignore a left turn on top of the mountain and descend toward Richmond on what, by now, is called Lenox Rd. At the bottom of the hill, pass a pond right, then curve right, leading to East Rd. Park more or less immediately, safely off the pavement, turn around and walk up.

EAST ROAD

The mountains and valley along Swamp Rd., from W. Stockbridge up through Richmond, are sparsely populated and lovely. The walk on East Rd. (mostly gravel) is a stroll from and to nowhere in particular, although if you were ambitious, you could make a loop of it as explained below. Here's a simple out and back on East Rd.: the views of enormous farm fields and the Taconic Hills to the west are interestingly different when walking in each direction. Because the mountain rises sharply on the east side of this walk, if you want sunshine, hold off until midday. Sunsets from here are dramatic.

The walk to the other end of East Rd., at Swamp Rd., is as long, short, slow or fast as you like. An estimated 2.3 mi. takes you to Swamp Rd., and so the full round trip is about 4.6 mi. The last part of East Rd. is in a woodsy residential area with some sweet country homes but no views. One highly unusual dome house can be seen about halfway out, right. You may want to walk only until the views disappear, then turn around to head back. You can picnic at roadside by the farm fields, but there are no facilities.

To make a loop: turn left on Swamp Rd. at the end of East Rd., and head S. to Lenox Rd., where you turn left again and spy your waiting car. Add 2 mi.

PERU

Peru is the highest town, in terms of elevation, in the county (and therefore the state), at 2,064 ft. It was incorporated July 4, 1771, as Partridgefield, because Oliver Partridge was one of the original purchasers of the grant. It began as a stop on a Boston to Albany stage line. The town was renamed in 1806, just two years after its western end had been lopped off to become Hinsdale, because like the country of Peru, it was in the mountains. And like the other Berkshire hilltowns, it subsisted on thin-soiled agriculture and a few mills, until young people heard of the kind of soil they grew out west. Then as now, residents went down to work in the more urban area of Pittsfield. With a population of under 810 and no shopping center, it remains one of the smallest Berkshire County towns. Few accommodations are available.

A 300-acre sanctuary near the center of town provides some excellent strolling.

WALK

RICE SANCTUARY

Various trails available

Road approaches

Take Rte. 8 to Hinsdale; turn E. on Rte. 143 to the center of town, recognizable because of the church on the left and the road junction. Turn right on South Rd. for .8 mi., then right again on Rice Rd.

DOROTHY FRANCES RICE SANCTUARY

The sign welcomes you to the Dorothy Frances Rice Sanctuary, provided you arrive during daylight hours from May 28 to October 12. Local people also ski there in the winter. The small building is a visitors' center. Nearby most of the trails come together, their arrows color coded, at a busy sign. Choose your color and follow in the direction of the arrow, because the trees are only "blazed," with colored blocks of wood, on one side. In other words, if you go the "wrong" way you won't see any blazes — although, for that matter, the trails are easy to follow, sections even mowed.

Dorothy Frances Rice died of tuberculosis shortly after graduating from Smith College, in Northampton. She loved this site of the family summer home. After her father, architect Orville Rice of New York City, died, her mother, Mary Rice, set up a trust to maintain the 300-acre property named for her daughter. The family home partly burned and was partly chewed down by voracious porcupines.

People in Peru still talk about two Smith College girls who lived in the visitors' center for one or more summers while studying the plants and animals. Eventually the trust turned the property over to the New England Forestry Foundation, together with an endowment. In season, a caretaker comes for two days a week to maintain the trails and the building. Witness 72-year-old Mel Fassell of Pittsfield, who was himself caretaker of the property for a stretch of 25 years.

Choose your color and follow your trail. Although as many as 1,500 people a year wander through the sanctuary, you probably won't see any of them. For the most part, the trails pass through old field growth laced with stone walls. The lengths of the walks vary and, of course, it is possible to connect them in different ways as they cross each other. Figure on 30 min. to an hr. — more if you want. Yes, those are bear scratches on the shed, for the Peru wilderness is alive with fauna as well as flora.

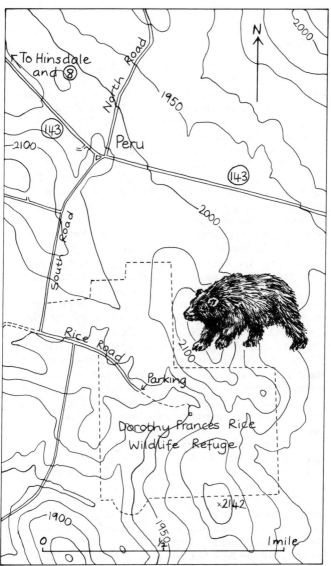

PERU: RICE SANCTUARY

PITTSFIELD

Solomon and Sarah Deming arrived from Wethersfield, Connecticut, at what's presently Elm St. and built their first home in 1752. They were Pontoosuc's first European settlers and their daughter, Dorothy, the first child of European extraction born in this wilderness. The other earliest residents were also from Connecticut, which was true in much of western Massachusetts. Settlers gathered in sufficient numbers over the next year to discuss founding a town and building a meeting house, located beside what became Park Square. They decided to name the town for William Pitt, English statesman who befriended the colonies and whose birthday was the same as the day in April, 1761 that Berkshire County split off from Hampshire County. Pittsfield was to become the shire town or county seat of Berkshire.

In 1764, Rev. Thomas Allen became the first minister, later accompanying the troops to the Battle of Bennington (1777), as the "Fighting Parson." The elm next to the first meeting house was spared in the construction of the second church, the one Charles Bulfinch designed, by the intercession of Lucretia Williams. Loyal to the king like her father, Israel Williams, she married the ardent patriot John Williams (no relation; every fourth person in western Massachusetts in those days was named Williams). Yet she survived and their marriage survived. At least they had plenty to talk about, and in 1783, when the peace was signed, they threw a party that, judging from contemporary accounts, may scarcely have been equaled since.

The elm, although struck by lightning, lived into the days Herman Melville spent in Pittsfield. He described scarred Capt. Ahab in terms of that tree, "greenly alive but branded." It finally had to be removed in 1864.

Poet Oliver Wendell Holmes's great-grandfather, Jacob Wendell, who originally bought the land for Pittsfield in 1736, drove a wonderful "one-hoss shay," subject of the poem "The Deacon's Masterpiece." That shay now sits in the basement of the Berkshire Museum, on South St., together with many other artifacts from the city's literary, historic, natural, and artistic past. O.W. Holmes's property is now owned by the Massachusetts Audubon Society, called as it always has been, Canoe Meadows. It is located where Pomeroy Ave. meets Holmes Rd.: Holmes Rd. being also the address of Melville's Pittsfield home, "Arrowhead" — now the headquarters of the Berkshire County Historical Society. The poet Henry Wadsworth Longfellow, of "Hiawatha" fame, stayed at the Dutch Colonial mansion built in 1781 by Henry Van Schaack, now the Pittsfield Country Club.

This building on Rte. 7, south of town, originally known as Broad Hall, was also the home for nine years of Elkanah Watson, who married science with agriculture in Berkshire. The merino sheep he imported changed the nature of farming in the county; the agricultural fairs he founded still continue in some form or other throughout western Massachusetts.

Another application of science created the modern city, which in the 19th century was smaller than its North County rival, No. Adams. In 1907 the General Electric Company established its plant in Pittsfield. A city that took 150 years to gain a population of 25,000, doubled that in the next 30 years. (And continued growing to near 58,000 in 1960. It has declined since.)

Early industries used water for paper and waterpower. As well as drawing from the Housatonic River and its tributaries, industries enlarged two lakes, Onota and Pontoosuc, as water reservoirs. Both now serve as recreational bases. Public swimming is available at Burbank Park on Onota and at the park just off Rte. 7 on Hancock Rd. for Pontoosuc. A city of nearly 50,000 once more, 36 percent of the entire county, Pittsfield is refreshed by its lakes and keeps its eye on the hills that surround it.

WALKS

DOWNTOWN

8 blocks (30 minutes)

Most of the walks in this book are in the country, many on trails. Nevertheless, cities in Berkshire County, even the largest, are not far removed from landscape. In fact, the view from the top floor of the Berkshire Plaza Hotel (corner of South and West streets) rivals that of many ridges. Another kind of view exists, however: that of the manmade attributes of Berkshire. This book attempts to capture some of the history of the county at all sites while walking: here in Pittsfield it's appropriate to take a downtown tour. The map of "Pittsfield: A Self-Guided Historic Walking Tour" is available for 25 cents at the Local History Room of the Berkshire Athenaeum, the modern building at the corner of Wendell and East streets.

The Athenaeum itself, with its Local Authors' Room, Children's Room, and Herman Melville Room, should be a stop on the tour. The map suggests that you start your trip at the Berkshire Museum, on South St. just beyond Park Square. This triple-threat museum, founded in 1903 by the son of the founder of the Dalton paper mills, contains art, history, and natural history. It runs a film and lecture series in its Little Cinema and other educational programs. Here are some of the highlights of the rest of the tour.

The map takes you past a series of buildings along Park Square, including the old Athenaeum, built in "Venetian Gothic Revival" style in 1876. It makes a statement, right? No longer a library, it now serves as the county district attorney's office and the mid-county registry of deeds. At the county surveyor's office on the first floor you can purchase the latest edition of the official county road map, an invaluable tool for locating the out-of-the-way, yet attractive enough to be framed.

In 1868 the then town of Pittsfield ended a 60-year struggle with Lenox about which was the appropriate town for the county seat by offering to build the Berkshire County Court House, next door. The state legislature then agreed to move the seat to the suitably gussied up building the town provided.

St. Stephen's Church, directly across the square from Wendell St., English Gothic in style, was built in 1889. As well as being architecturally interesting to visit, informal sandwich lunches are available for a small charge in the basement in the summer.

Across the street from St. Stephen's stands the elegant town hall, built in 1832. After years as a civic center, it is now used for offices. Next, to the west, the First Church of Christ, Congregational, built in 1853, incorporates clock, bell, and bootscraper from a Charles Bulfinch–designed predecessor built in 1793. This substantial building serves as a reminder that from Colonial days right through to mid-19th century, church and state were one in Massachusetts.

The Berkshire Bank (formerly the Berkshire County Savings Bank), at the North St. corner, was built in 1894. In the warmer weather, it shares the site with its trademark, the popcorn wagon. The popper, now operated electrically, was once driven by steam. The wagon, which has stood on the corner since 1910, is on the National Register of Historic Places. The Berkshire Corner, across North St., was built in 1868 as the headquarters for Berkshire Life Insurance Co., now located in the imposing building across from the country club on South St.

The Trust Company of Berkshire, just north of the popcorn bank, now headquarters of the Bank of New England-West, was built in 1923 in a classical revival style. BankBoston, farther down the same side of the street, also looks just like a bank, although more distinctly Greek. The tour map notes that this is one of the few buildings on North St. that has all four sides exposed, while much of the street is a continuous wall of fronts.

The Rosa England block, just across Fenn St. and now known as the Galleria, is one of Pittsfield's Victorian buildings. Although the facade has been adapted to the 20th century, most of the elegant features were preserved. The flatiron-shaped Eagle Building at the corner of Eagle St. (1904) is as efficient a use of available space next to the railroad tracks as you could find. Although the newspaper itself has moved to larger quarters in a former mill, on So. Church St., the city is the richer for this distinctive structure and the sightly vest-pocket park that fills the tip of the triangle.

In a slight departure from the prescribed route, you might want to head E. on Eagle St. and then S. on Renne St., to pass the home of the Berkshire Artisans and take a gander at the mural that decorates the wall. The First United Methodist Church at the corner of Fenn replaces a wooden structure that partially burned in 1871. The chancel window was created by Tiffany of New York.

The city government buildings are located to the south of Fenn St. The city hall moved into the white Vermont marble, classic building in 1967. It was built as a post office in 1910. The Central Fire Station, just beyond, on the National Register of Historic Places, was built in 1895. The next year the city purchased horses to pull the heavy engines.

From here it is a short walk, continuing in the same direction, back to Park Square, with its distinctive veterans' memorial, a map of Southeast Asia.

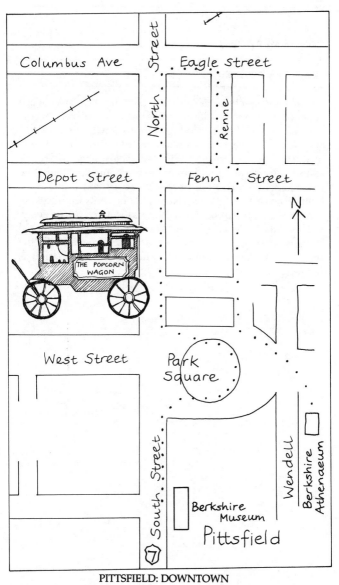

PITTSFIELD: DOWNTOWN

CANOE MEADOWS

Various trails available

This Massachusetts Audubon Sanctuary consists of 262 acres of wetlands bordering the Housatonic River. Access is from Holmes Rd. just to the N. of its junction with Pomeroy Ave. The property, with its 3 mi. of trails, is open 9 a.m. to dusk, Tuesday through Sunday. The foliage filters the sound of traffic and the sight of nearby homes, so that while in a residential area, the property carries you to the open fields of an earlier Pittsfield. No rest rooms, but outhouses are available. A blind to observe wildlife is located on a causeway. The essentially level trails across meadows and occasional bridges are skiable as long as wet areas are frozen under the snow. There is a self-guided nature tour. A donation is requested from non-members.

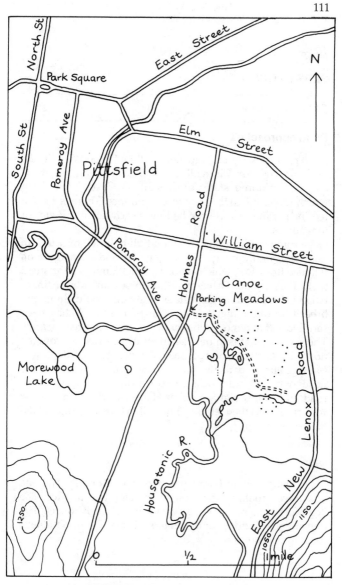

PITTSFIELD: CANOE MEADOWS

HIKE

BERRY POND

5 miles (2 hours)

Road approaches

From Park Square, Pittsfield, follow W. on West St., 2.5 mi.; turn right on Churchill St. for 1.25 mi.; and left at the chocolate-colored state forest sign on Cascade St. from which it is .5 mi. to the state forest entrance. There is a small fee for parking, to use the bathing beach at Lulu Pond, or for camping.

From the north, turn right on Bull Hill Rd., off Rte. 7 in Lanesborough, and go .5 mi.; jog left and then right on Balance Rock Rd., which swings S. for 1.3 mi. to a Pittsfield State Forest gate. Drive in .5 mi. to see an extraordinary balanced rock, on so delicate a base you would think any breeze would blow it over. The painted rock has been sandblasted to remove fools' names, which have reappeared. The rock is what is known as an erratic, carried in from the north by a glacier and deposited when the ice departed. Many trails lead to the part of the forest where you are headed, but consider Balance Rock a side trip; drive out the road and follow right to either Hancock Rd. or Causeway; turn right and then left on Churchill to Cascade; right at the State Forest sign.

Camping

Pittsfield State Forest has two campgrounds. The one at Parker Brook, to the west of the HQ, has 18 sites. The "comfort station," in state parlance, has flush toilets. The one at Berry Pond, your destination, 13 sites, with pit toilets, meaning outhouses.

BERRY POND

This is a moderately steep hike, passing the common corner of the towns of Pittsfield, Lanesborough, and Hancock — where Berry Pond is actually located in Pittsfield State Forest. You pass through some extraordinary azalea fields, which bloom in early June; by a fine overlook into New York State; and to Berry Pond, elevation 2,060 ft., the highest natural body of water in Massachusetts. (The highest, at 3,200 ft., is on Mt. Greylock, dug as water supply for Bascom Lodge.)

Because the blazing and signing of trails at Pittsfield has been erratic, you may wish to stop in at forest HQ to pick up the latest map or to inquire about the route. The problem is a bewildering excess of trails. From the state forest entrance it's .5 mi. to Lulu Pond picnic area, where you park — and where you may want to swim or at least wade at the end of the hike. Cross the road from the parking lot. Take Honwee Trail, the second below the gate, a woods road. It is blazed yellow, parallel to and only a few feet above the Lulu Brook Trail and the Berry Pond Circuit Rd. It is pleasant to look down at the brook itself as you pass through beech, maple, and birch forest, with azaleas prominent on the understory or lower foliage.

Ignore the water supply road that comes in right in a few min. and continue on a moderately rising trail — a wet, salamander heaven. It shows the marks of trail bikes in its ruts. Ignore another trail from the right at 23 min. You pass through a stand of pines. At a major intersection 15 min. later, turn left across the brook and then up Berry Pond Circuit Rd. Although the traffic can be heavy on a weekend during azalea season, the shoulders are walkable. The three towns come together just south of the road at about this point.

At 43 min. on a sharp curve to the SE, the Taconic Skyline Trail, blazed white, exits the road, right. To the left is your first chance to get on Turner Trail. Or, stay on road. You walk into the overlook at 52 min. The mountains before you are the Catskills. Berry Pond, surrounded by tent sites, is 3 min. ahead.

Backtrack to the Turner Trail, or follow trails on either side of the pond (trails may be wet). Either way, you will end up on the Turner, heading SSE. It is or has been blazed red, but not consistently. At first it passes along a plateau but eventually begins to descend steeply, crossed by trails at 10, 15, and 36 min. This last you can take as a shortcut back to the up-traffic side of the Circuit Rd.

These are all well-used trails, so you may want to choose weekdays, when the 4-wheelers are less likely to be prowling.

If you continue on Turner, at 40 min. turn left on a gravel road; then left again on Circuit Rd. after 5 min. In 4 more min. you will be back at the parking lot, ready for a dip.

Many other combinations of trails are possible. The route described here is skiable, as are many of the other trails and unplowed roads. One special trail at Pittsfield State Forest is wheelchair accessible, the Tranquility Trail, west of the HQ building.

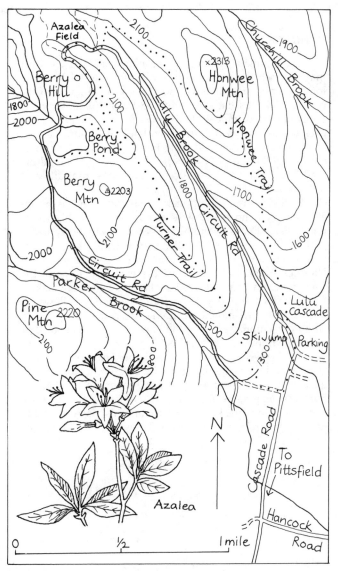

Azalea Field

Churchill Brook
1900

× 2313

Honwee Mtn

2100

Berry Hill
1800
2000

Lulu Brook

Honwee Trail

2100

Berry Pond

Berry Mtn
2203

1800

1700

Circuit Rd

1600

Turner Trail

2100

2000

Circuit Rd

Parker Brook

Pine Mtn
2220
2100

1500

Lulu Cascade

Ski Jump

Parking

1300

N

Azalea

To Pittsfield

Cascade Road

Hancock Road

0   ½   1 mile

PITTSFIELD: BERRY POND

HANCOCK

On the map, Hancock looks like what was left over maybe when the rest of Berkshire County was laid out: a long, narrow strip along the northwestern boundary of the county and thus the state, running from Williamstown to Richmond. It is impossible to drive from one end of Hancock to the other within the town lines. Six thousand acres of mountainous Pittsfield State Forest intervene. The three sections of the town of 640, north, village, and Shaker, draw mail from different post offices, draw wires from different utilities, and pledge different loyalties.

Settled in pre-Revolutionary times, the town was originally called Jericho, because the steep slopes were likened to the walls Joshua sent tumbling. When it was incorporated in 1776, it was named for the patriot whose large signature decorates the Declaration of Independence, John Hancock. Samuel Hand, who represented the town in the state government in the 1790s, asked his fellow lawmakers for hazardous duty pay — or at least a clothing allowance — because "the mountains are so steep that one can not climb out without spoiling the knees of his pantaloons, or go back without spoiling his seat."

The biggest business by far is Jiminy Peak, once solely a ski area and now a mountain resort. The second largest business is the not-for-profit Hancock Shaker Village. Second home developments are rising. A few farms, a few stores, some bed and breakfasts and restaurants, as well as the more commercial area along Rte. 20 out of Pittsfield, make up the rest of town.

HIKE

SHAKER MOUNTAIN

6.5 miles (3 hours)

Road approaches

From Park Square in Pittsfield follow Rte. 20 W. for 5 mi. Park in the lot for Hancock Shaker Village, on your left across the Hancock town line.

Most people taking this hike will want to tour Hancock Shaker Village first, to learn about the souls who built the industrial and holy sites you are about to visit. The Shaker religion reached its zenith in this country in the 1830s. These celibates believed that all work was an expression of God's glory; thus their furniture and craftsmanship are both simple and exquisite. A tour of 20 restored buildings, including crafts workshops and the famous round barn, takes at least 2 hrs. There is a fee. The village is open May through October, 9:30 a.m. to 5 p.m. The Visitors' Center, adjacent to the parking lot, contains rest rooms, lunch shop, information center, and museum shop. Picnic tables are available. Nearest camping is at Pittsfield State Forest.

SHAKER MOUNTAIN

'Tis a gift to be simple
'Tis a gift to be free
'Tis a gift to come down
Where you want to be. . . . — Shaker hymn

The first simple gift you will receive from the Shakers, or at least the non-profit corporation that runs their village, is the absence of a fee for taking this hike. You will receive other gifts. Nevertheless, because the first part of it is on village property (the rest is in Pittsfield State Forest), as a courtesy tell the folks at the Visitors' Center where you are going. This remarkable hike takes you past the unrestored remains of the North Family or industrial grouping of Hancock Shakers. Included is the village's water system, mill sites, dams, the foundations of a residence, 150-year-old cart roads, charcoal-burning sites, stone walls, and hilltop holy sites of both the Hancock village and the New Lebanon (New York) Shaker Village. After that, with any luck at all, you will come down where you want to be, right where you started.

Use the crosswalk to get to the north side of Rte. 20 and to the fields behind the 1793 Meeting House, the most westerly of the village buildings. Head N. (it may be necessary to detour stock enclosures) to the logging road. The trail departs N. from a cleared log landing 2 min. from the highway. Laid out by the Boy Scouts, it is marked by green triangles with white circles. Even if these have not been kept up, you begin on an unmistakable cart road that soon follows the western side of Shaker Brook. The stone walls may have been laid up in 1845. Eight min. from the high way you arrive at the lower dam, the beginning of a sophisticated water system. The pipe fills a reservoir from which it traveled underground to the village where it first powered machinery, then supplied the wash rooms, then the stables, then the mills, and then the fields to water the cattle. The old bridge above the dam has been replaced. Cross.

As you follow down the eastern side of the stream you pass first an industrial site with a pit for a water wheel and then the cellar hole for the North Family residence. To imagine its size, compare with the Brick Dwelling in the village, although this one was made of wood. At 15 min. into the walk, not counting the time you have taken to examine the ruins, turn left up the hill, through second-growth hardwood with some shagbark hickory and hemlock, on what was probably the Shakers' original cart road to their holy site.

At 27 min. bear left where a branch of the road continues straight. This was a charcoal-burning site. At 34 min. cross under power lines that serve airplane beacon lights for the Pittsfield airport. You switch back to cross under the lines again.

At 44 min. you enter the overgrown field that was the Hancock Shakers' holy ground, which they called Mt. Sinai, now referred to as Shaker Mtn. The Shakers did not permit non-believers on this site. In 1841 or 1842, all Shaker communities were required to clear the summit of a nearby hill, focusing on a "fountain" or hexagonal fence surrounding a marble slab, about which they marched, sang, and danced in May and September. A depression in the blackberry bushes beside the trail marks the fountain; little else remains at Mt. Sinai; more artifacts are visible at Holy Mount, about a mile as the bird flies across the valley. Shakers called to each other across the chasm.

The trail follows along the ridge and then turns left, into the valley. At about 50 min., it switches back through a lovely hemlock grove. At 1:03 you come out on a lumber road. Turn left. If you wish a 1:30 min. hike, follow straight back to the village. Otherwise turn right almost immediately. This road follows to the left of a stone wall. At the end of the wall (1:18), bear left down the hill. The trail swings right, between sections of a different stone wall and across a brook (1:23). The forest in this section has not been lumbered as ruthlessly as has the forest in the valley and on Shaker Mtn. Follow up the hill to a junction of walls and trails (1:27), where you turn left, again following a stone wall.

At 1:36 pass an opening in the wall that probably admitted a cart road from the New Lebanon community to its holy ground. At 1:41 you arrive at what was a gated entrance, elevation 1,927 ft. (higher than Mt. Sinai). Follow the wall, on the inside, left to the feast ground and the foundations of the shelter (1:44). Although the Shakers planted a row of pines around each site, the CCC planted the pine trees inside, in the 1930s. If you head into the woods directly in front of the shelter, you may find the depression in the ground that marks the fountain site. There was an altar 10 yds. west of the fountain.

Downhill from the alter is a beautiful specimen of the wall-maker's art, probably one day's labor, 3 feet at the base and tapering to the top, 18 feet long. The brethren must have taken 350 man-days to build the wall around the sacred lot, not to mention the other walls you have seen.

Starting in front of the shelter, head W., bearing right downhill on a trail that reaches an opening in the wall (1:53). Although the path generally follows the wall to the left, it swings out in an arc before rejoining at the corner. This section of trail, which is not based on an old road and has not experienced much wear, is hard to follow even with the markers. The corner of the wall encloses a natural amphitheater (2:03), containing a spring. If you did not stop to picnic at either summit, this would be a good spot. Cross the brook below the corner and follow steeply up the hill, along the path, until it comes out on a fire road (2:20). Turn left. The brook is on your right. You pass the first of several wide spots on the road, which were charcoal-burning sites. You may find some pieces of charcoal. Follow the fire road until it turns left, uphill, while the older cart road you continue straight to a brook crossing (2:29). From here follow the green triangle down the branch of the brook to take in a Shaker marble quarry.

At 2:41 you return to the main cart road (bear right) at the site of the high dam, which is largely washed out. It may have been constructed in 1810. Just below, the Shakers built a sawmill that bridged the stream. Logs were loaded at the retaining wall on the far side. The depressions on the near side were mill foundations. This mill, which ran on water power or steam when water wasn't sufficient, was built mid-19th century and burned in 1926.

Follow the cart road to the log landing. Total round trip is just about 3 hrs., counting only travel time. It would be possible to ski Shaker Mtn. but not Holy Mount. A ski loop, the same as for an abbreviated hike, would return via the lumber road you meet after descending Shaker Mtn.

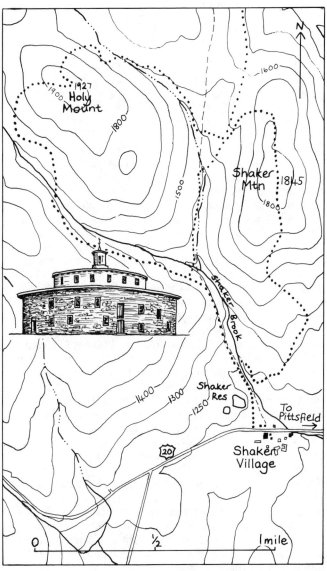

1927
Holy
Mount

Shaker
Mtn · 1845

1600

1800

1500

1800

Shaker Brook

1400   1300   Shaker
Res
1250

To
Pittsfield →

20

Shaker
Village

N

0   ½   1 mile

HANCOCK: SHAKER MOUNTAIN

DALTON

A town of about 7,077 population at a junction of Rtes. 8 and 9, east of Pittsfield, Dalton has been dominated by paper manufacturing virtually since its incorporation in 1784. It is still a paper town. In 1799 Henry Wiswell, John Willard, and Zenas Crane began a mill on the Housatonic that produced the first paper made in Berkshire County. The history of the forerunners of Crane & Co. is one of rapid technological progress and spectacular fires. Local residents attributed the success of the company in part to the quality of a spring on the premises. Early on, the company made collars, bond, bank notes, and parchment; now it is best known for manufacturing the paper on which the U.S. currency is printed. The Crane Paper Museum on Rte. 9, west of town, portrays the history of paper-making; additional artifacts are exhibited at the Berkshire Museum in Pittsfield.

Because the AT passes through town, Dalton is well known to through-hikers as a pleasant and friendly stop, with an array of places to eat and stay along the main street.

Wahconah Brook falls near the Windsor border. It was known to Indians but "discovered" by William Cleveland while he was looking for a beehive. He built a dam above the falls and a flume around them to drop the water on the overshot wheel of a grist mill, about 1770. His mill-stones were fashioned in France and hauled to the site by boat to Boston and oxen across the Bay Colony. About 1800 Jacob Booth added a sawmill to the site.

As is true of other county falls and cliffs, Wahconah Falls comes with an assortment of Indian traditions. In one story, Wahconah, denied a suitor from an enemy tribe, jumped into the brook. In another, Wahconah, whose father was a prominent chief, said she would marry the brave who could leap across the chasm above the falls, which was narrower in those days. Of the two who made the attempts the wrong one cleared and the right one landed in the brook. So she jumped in after him and they went over the falls together to their deaths.

WALK

WAHCONAH FALLS

A few hundred feet

The popular waterfall and gorge is located at Wahconah Falls State Park on Rte. 9 in Dalton. Coming from Dalton center, turn right at the sign, passing Dalton Tractor. About a mi. up gravel Wahconah Rd. lies the parking lot. No fee, no camping, no lifeguard, but a composting toilet. A sometime party spot, at last visit it had accumulated a good deal of trash. It is hard to understand why the public can't treat a beautiful resource with respect. On this 53-acre tract you will find a deep gulf, rocky ledges, large hemlocks, and a scattering of picnic grills. Trails meander through the woods on either side of the brook. The falls dive deeply over ledges below Windsor Reservoir on a tributary of the Housatonic. Deep pools below beckon the visitor who wants to cool off — strictly at your own risk, of course. (For map, see Dalton-Windsor map under "Windsor Jambs.")

WINDSOR

Once Plantation No. 4, the land making up Windsor was sold to a consortium of buyers in 1762, prototypes of today's land developers: buy a chunk of wilderness, survey it, and try to sell the lots for a good profit. The boundaries weren't exactly the same, including then part of present day Dalton and Cheshire but not the present northern part of Windsor — which was considered a section of plantation No. 5, Cummington (in Hampshire County).

As sometimes happens to developers even now, the lots moved slowly, which made it hard for the consortium to pay off its notes; furthermore, many of those who bought were also speculators rather than pioneers, so time passed before any significant settlement. Still, in 1771, residents petitioned to incorporate as Gageborough, after the pre-Revolutionary governor of the colony. In 1777 they petitioned to change the name, British Gen. Gage having fallen out of favor in 1775. By the end of that century, the area was a thriving farming community, with the usual accumulation of mills. When the sons and daughters of farmers went west and when the railroad failed to pass through town, Windsor became a byway.

By the beginning of the 20th century, Gen. Alfred E. Bates had begun accumulating former farms in the north of town, while Helen Gamwell Ely was accumulating land to the south to form her Helenscourt. In the 1920s, Elizabeth C.T. Miller bought the Bates estate. Mrs. Ely remarried Lt. Col. Arthur D. Budd, who also acquired the Miller property. Thus, the 3,000 acres of Notchview Reservation, nearly a quarter of the town, resulted from the union of two large estates, located on Rte. 9. Now owned by TTOR, Notchview borders 1,616 acres of Windsor State Forest and is nearby a similar-sized tract that is part of the state forest and part of a Wildlife Management Area, presumably fixing the character of the town for some time to come.

Camping

Camping is available for a small fee in season at Windsor Jambs State Park, part of the state forest. The area is just E. and N. of Notchview, on River Rd. (signs on Rte. 116 and Rte. 9 direct you to the park). A foot trail along Steep Bank Brook connects the Jambs with Notchview, about 3.0 mi. to the Budd Visitors' Center. At the campground, a stream is dammed for swimming. Tourist accommodations are not available in Windsor.

WALKS

WINDSOR JAMBS

3 miles (1.5 hours)

When people talk about the Jambs, they mean the state park with its swimming area (follow the signs from Rtes. 116 or 9). Strictly speaking, however, the Jambs is (are) a nearby gorge, the name derived perhaps from the stream's narrowed route through a rock doorway. Park in the lot by park HQ. Across the road, generally bear right through the camping area for the Jambs Trail, which actually begins behind the toilet building. You can also drive to the scenic gorge on the gravel Lower Rd., but to do so would be to miss out on a 3-mi., round-trip stroll through a deep ever-green forest. The leisurely path, blazed blue, wanders in its own insouciant way through spruce, hemlock, and even some pine and fir. The trail is wet and, as it runs beside the Jambs, requires sure-footedness, so wear hiking shoes. For the best effect, at the junction follow the trail to the lower Jambs, then work up along the edge, protected by the fence, to upper Jambs. The trail back leaves from the parking lot. Jambs Brook has cut deeply into slabs of rock, tumbling over many small falls, a pleasing sight even when, in midsummer, not much water passes through.

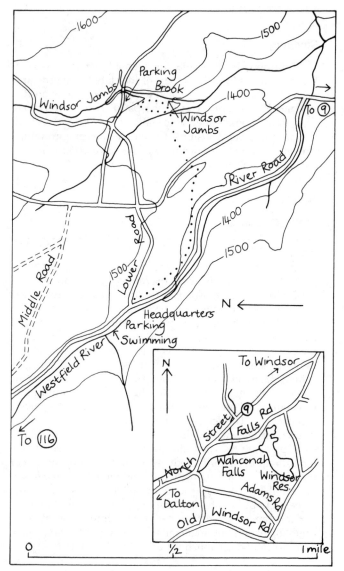

DALTON – WINDSOR: WAHCONAH FALLS / WINDSOR JAMBS

HIKE

NOTCHVIEW / JUDGE'S HILL

5.5 miles (2.25 hours)

Road approaches

Take Rte. 9 E. from Pittsfield, through Dalton, and up the long hill to Windsor. The entrance to Notchview is 1 mi. E. of the junction with Rte. 8-A (N.). That road, recently rebuilt after years of axle bending, drops S. from Rte. 116 out of Adams, an alternate course for people setting sail from north county.

JUDGE'S HILL

The Arthur D. Budd Visitors' Center, at the parking lot, serves as an information booth and provides a place for cross-country skiers to wax and warm. Restrooms are available. There are picnic tables and there is a water source, but no camping is allowed.

TTOR maintains this 3,000-acre reservation, which takes its name from the view from Lt. Col. Budd's former home through a notch eastward into the hills of Cummington. Rte. 9 passes through the Notch. Budd, a World War II hero, donated the property in 1965. The Trustees charge a nominal fee to non-members for use. The property shows traces of farming the soil of these hills, known as "rock farming," and of the later era of gentlemen's estates.

The 25 mi. of trails on the property pass through trees that have grown up on former fields — and also some fields that are cut. Although you only climb 297 ft. to the summit of Judge's Hill, the highest land in Windsor, you start at an elevation of 2,000 ft. This quality of highland plateau, complete with evergreen forests, harsh climate, rocky soil, bogs, and deep stream crevasses, distinguishes Notchview. Wildlife here includes white-tail deer, bobcat, nesting hawks, and occasional bear.

You may choose any combination of a multitude of

well-marked and well-maintained trails. As a 5.5-miler, for instance, for a morning's hike (or ski), walk straight ahead from the parking area, leaving the barn on the left, and turning left on the Circuit Trail. You walk gently up through a wet, spruce area. At 12 min., turn left on Judge's Hill Trail. (All Notchview trails are blazed yellow; however, ample signs let you know which one you're on.) At first you lose elevation, crossing Shaw Rd. (gravel) and descending through mixed hardwoods and across a bridge. Then you begin to climb moderately, through an area marked by large glacial boulders.

After 31 min. you achieve the summit, marked by the stone remains of the fireplace of the Judge's "fort," laid up without mortar. Most of the surrounding growth is quite young; he must have had a marvelous view when the land was cleared. Judge James M. Barker was the most prominent member of a social and sporting group known as the Windsor Club, which held weekend hunting and fishing trips on the property. He erected the stone lunch stop, walled around and complete with stone tables and benches, about the turn of the century.

It takes 9 min. to descend to Bates Rd., a gravel surface on which you turn right. You pass between the cellar holes and stone walls of some of the 2 dozen families who at one time lived in the area. In one, a rabbit warren has been cleverly burrowed under a concrete slab. Is this the site of the Babbitt Axe Factory? Could these be the Babbitt rabbits? The Steep Bank Brook Trail, which departs left, would take you to Windsor Jambs.

Pick up the Bumpus Trail, left, through open fields past a shelter to the Gen. Bates homesite. He fought Indians in Kansas and Wyoming. His cousin, Herman, was famous for the quality of the butter he produced on this highland farm, becoming known as Butter Bates. The open fields provide a nice contrast to traveling the woods. The Bumpus trail turns abruptly right, crossing Shaw Rd. (1:14) and descending steeply into a gorge. It crosses a bridge over Shaw Brook, then climbs through evergreens. Continue straight at the Y, 9 min. later. Follow the signs towards the Visitors' Center,

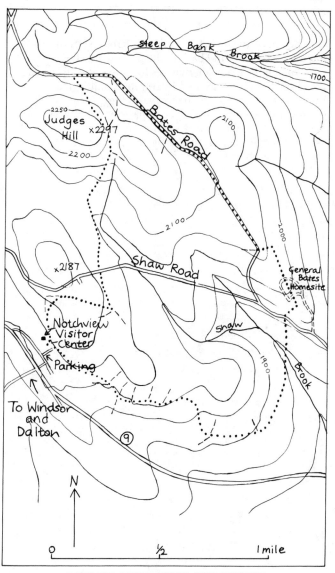

WINDSOR: NOTCHVIEW / JUDGE'S HILL

coming out on the open Sawmill Field, crossing it, and picking up the Circuit Trail back to the parking lot (1:55).

Among the many alternatives for walks as well as hikes
is the mile-long, self-guided interpretive trail in the Hume
Brook area at Notchview that explains the principles of forest land management, with an emphasis on forest aesthetics
and wildlife. TTOR issues separate maps for hiking and
skiing; a large map is posted by the parking lot. Bring a
picnic; spend the day.

NORTH COUNTY

CHESHIRE

Cheshire in early days was called New Providence by homesick Rhode Islanders. Col. Joab Stafford led a group of his townspeople to the Battle of Bennington on August 15, 1777. A monument and a Wildlife Management Area honor him. In 1801 the town combined all its milk production for one day into a 1,255-pound cheese, which oxen dragged to a boat on the Hudson River and thence to Washington to honor newly elected President Thomas Jefferson. Most of the Cheshire lakes, the headwaters of the Hoosic River, falling within the town borders, were dammed to provide a head at low water for the former Adams Print Works. The AT crosses the river and Rte. 8 in town on its way to climb into the Mt. Greylock State Reservation via Outlook Ave. Many through-hikers on the trail stop in Cheshire to pick up mail forwarded to them c/o General Delivery at the post office and to sleep at a friendly church.

WALK

HOOSIC RIVER RAILROAD

Adams and Cheshire, 4.5 miles (2 hours)

You need not worry about trains along this section of roadbed, although in the mid-19th century the Hoosic River Railroad was an important artery. Now it is a wonderful, water-level route, primarily frequented by four-legged game and waterfowl. A group is attempting to establish the Ashawilticook Trail along it.

This walk is best enjoyed by using 2 cars. Leave auto No. 1 at the dead end of Grove St. just north of the Rte. 8 overpass in the south end of Adams (the idea is to have the car on the same side of the river as the roadbed). Park No. 2 at the Rte. 8 roadside rest beside the reservoir. Take off on the roadbed south of the restaurant at the nearby grade crossing, by the reservoir dam. Cross the bridge over Kitchen Brook. You pass by some back yards with barking dogs. Play the part of the train as you cross Church St. Soon you are removed from houses and dogs, as South Brook enters from the southeast. Stafford Hill rises northeast and the Greylock massif, northwest.

Natives call this section the Jungle, as the 10-ft.-wide Hoosic writhes through swampland. Alligators you need not worry about; however, nesting snapping turtles can be a problem in late spring. The calcareous (lime-based) wetlands west of the tracks, and marshes and shrub swamps east of the tracks, are fine habitat for a variety of water creatures. Wood duck platforms dot the wetlands, deer and muskrat tracks follow the stream. You may see snowshoe hare, pheasant, occasional fox, and some naturally reproducing brown trout as well as stocked trout. Note that although heading north, you are going downstream. Rte. 8 is close at hand, but not noticeable except for the distant sound of a truck downshifting. You see a gouged hillside of gravel pits to the left.

A brick building belonging to the town of Adams introduces the first road for 3 mi. This is the pumping station for 2 artesian wells. Around the corner appears a bridge. Although walking across is no problem, you may wonder if it is possible to ski the open trestle in winter. Yes, because skis nicely bridge the space between the ties.

Welcome to Cheshire Harbor, said to be named because it harbored runaway slaves, a lovely spot with an old swimming hole, somewhat silted in. Now the river is on the left, with Rte. 8 just the other side. You can see the stonework of a mill sluiceway. Follow the railroad under Rte. 8. On the other side you should see your car.

It would be possible to stroll from Coltsville in Pitts-

133

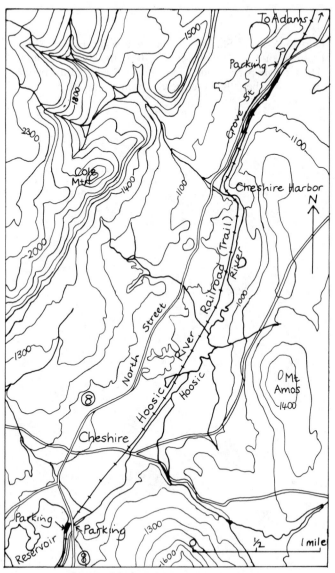

CHESHIRE: HOOSIC RIVER RAILROAD

field to Ashland St., No. Adams, where the Hoosic River Railroad joins the live one, coming from the Hoosac Tunnel. (Do not walk near tracks in use.) But you won't find a better stretch anywhere than the one you've just completed.

ADAMS AND MOUNT GREYLOCK

Adams, first East Township, then East Hoosuck, was finally named for Revolutionary War hero Samuel Adams in 1778. Its remarkable ethnic heritage began with English Quakers, whose vitality carved an industrial center from the wilderness, and continued through successive waves of immigrants who came to labor in those industries: Irish, Scots, Germans, French Canadians, and Poles. Although the textile mills have ceased and although its northern end was lopped off to form No. Adams, Adams remains a bustling town of 9,270, with all the accommodations and services a walker could want. Most stores and restaurants are along Rte. 8, which goes by different names such as Columbia and Park streets. The statue of William McKinley in front of the library honors a friend of a foremost Adams family, the Plunketts. McKinley's high tariff policies benefited the local cloth manufacturers.

Although the summit of Mt. Greylock lies in the town of Adams, the Mt. Greylock State Reservation encompasses 12,000 acres of hilly land in the towns of Adams, Cheshire, Lanesborough, New Ashford, No. Adams, and Williamstown. But you only have to look upwards in Adams to understand why the town feels a special regard for the mountain that looms over it. Mt. Greylock is a close, intimate friend.

Greylock is the tallest peak in southern New England at 3,491 feet. It is surrounded by half a dozen lower eminences, most of which are still higher than anything else in Massachusetts, Connecticut, and Rhode Island: Saddleball (3,238), Mt. Fitch (3,110), Mt. Williams (2,951), Mt. Prospect (2,690), Stony Ledge (2,580), and Ragged Mtn. (2,451).

So it is not as high as some of the Adirondacks or the White Mtns. or the Green Mtns. even — which you can see from Greylock. At one time the Appalachians, of which Greylock is a part, stood Himalayan high, six times their present altitude, but time and weather have eroded them. Even in the early 19th century, before the more spectacular, western scenery in this country was accessible, Greylock created a lot of excitement.

All the great American writers and naturalists, like Thoreau, Hawthorne, and Melville, made their pilgrimages to Greylock. The first person to publish an account of his visit, in 1800, was the former president of Yale, Timothy Dwight, who said "the view was immense and of amazing grandeur. . .". It inspired prose, poetry, fiction and energetic enjoyment of the out-of-doors.

A popular destination as it has been and still is, not surprisingly, the summit is reached by paved roads from No. Adams (Notch Rd.) and from Lanesborough (Rockwell Rd.), which meet a mile from the top, from where they travel together as Summit Rd. A gravel-surfaced road, known as New Ashford or Greylock, climbs from the west to Rockwell Rd. not far below a gravel spur known as Sperry Rd. This provides a way to the public campgrounds (which have no recreational vehicle hookups, showers, or flush toilets). Tent sites are distributed discreetly in a spruce grove. Stony Ledge, at the end of Sperry Rd., provides a spectacular view of the Hopper, a V-shaped wedge worn by erosion on the western side.

The summit has limited development, such as broadcast towers and communications dishes. A 100-ft.-high War Memorial Tower, a design similar to a proposal for a lighthouse in the Charles River estuary, 130 miles away, was erected on Greylock in the 1930s to pick up the spirits of local residents during hard times. The state-owned Bascom Lodge, built by the CCC during the New Deal and run by the AMC, provides modest accommodations and good, hearty food, in season (reservations required). The hikers' breakfasts and Tuesday evening barbecues are not to be missed. Enthusiastic interpreters lead walks and conduct programs to explain the natural and human history of the mountain.

A 7.8-mi. segment of the 2,050-mi.-long AT transects the reservation from S. to N., a ribbon that hangs over most of the peaks. Remember: the AT is blazed white. Of the 5 three-sided shelters on the reservation, two are associated with the AT. Ten side trails to the AT, blazed blue, together with 11 other trails and the AT, total 43 mi. of hiking in the Greylock range — routes shorter or longer, steeper or more gentle, fit just about every walker's time and ambition.

The War Memorial Tower, open during posted hours, extends the view from the summit to 70 or 100 miles in clear conditions. Innumerable more local views reveal Adams from the east of the summit, the farms of Williamstown from the trail intersection on Mt. Prospect, the peak itself from Ragged, the lakes and rounded hills of mid-Berkshire from Jones' Nose or Rounds' Rock.

Views on the mountains include tumbling streams. March Cataract flows best when the snows melt. You can see it from Rte. 7 in front of Mt. Greylock Regional High School. A trail from the campground leads to it. The Deer Hill Trail from the campground passes a falls on Roaring Brook. Money Brook Falls, also tucked into the Hopper, can be reached by a side trail to the Money Brook Trail.

Most of the vegetation on Greylock is northern hardwood: beech, birch, maple, and few evergreens. In the southern portions of the reservation, recent second growth fills formerly farmed fields. Here and there on the mountains' steep slopes stand aged trees, in areas not cut for railroads or other development over the years. Especially the 1,600 acres of the Hopper, on the west side, contain red spruce stands nearly 200 years old. The state has designated the Hopper a Natural Area. The federal government, together with the Society of American Foresters, has recognized these spruces as a National Natural Landmark. To protect the Hopper, it is a low-impact area, excluding vehicles, camp fires, and camping but available for study and hiking.

Its upper reaches are covered by a boreal type of balsam and yellow birch forest, probably the only example of such woods in Massachusetts. The bogs and stunted fir growth near the summits of Greylock and Saddleback are similar to the vegetation on the Canadian Shield — the fir forest of the far north. Your experience as a hiker arriving in them is exhilarating.

The variety of wildlife matches the diverse vegetation. Forty state-listed rare or endangered species have been seen on the reservation, as well as birds as unusual as Swainson's thrush and the blackpoll warbler. Viewers come to watch a variety of hawks performing their aerobatics by taking advantage of updrafts on the steepest part of the east face. Common wildlife include the whitetail deer, bobcat, snow shoe hare, cottontail rabbit, ruffed grouse, woodcock, raccoon, red squirrel, chipmunk, fox, skunk, woodchuck, and the porcupine that hang around the shelters to chew your hiking boots if you leave them unattended. Bear, the eastern coyote, wild turkey, fisher, and raven have recently returned to the reservation, as surrounding farm fields grow over.

Berkshire County is blessed by 150,000 acres of land protected from development, approximately one-quarter its total area. The Greylock Reservation stands as the flagship of the state's park system and as the jewel of the county's public and private holdings.

This book describes walks and hikes in the summit area, and in the campground area. The walks are the Overlook Trail, Stony Ledge, March Cataract, and Deer Hill. It describes 5 hikes: one from Notch Rd. in to the ridge of Prospect Mtn.; Cheshire Harbor Trail, from the southwest; Bellows Pipe Trail from the north; Hopper Trail from the west; and Stony Ledge/Roaring Brook from the southeast. Dogs are only allowed on leash at the campground.

WALKS

OVERLOOK TRAIL

2.5 miles (1 hour)

Try the Overlook Trail from the summit, fairly rigorous going that passes by fine overlooks into the Hopper. Depart from the television tower, except turn right instead of following the Hopper Trail. Descent is constant through mixed woods to Notch Rd. Cross it into the woods again at about 10 min., continuously losing altitude until the stream crossing just above March Cataract Falls (40 min.). The overlooks, down short trails, are in this vicinity. Shortly you come out on the Hopper Trail, at which you turn left to climb back up to the TV tower.

CAMPGROUND TRAILS

Stony Ledge, 2 miles; March Cataract, approximately 2 miles; Deer Hill, 2.25 miles

Several trails depart from the campground, including a self-guided nature and cultural walk. Consult the supervisor at the contact station for detailed information on their present state. The most spectacular is simply to continue up gravel Sperry Rd. 1.0 mi. from the contact station to Stony Ledge, with its breathtaking view over the sheer depths of the Hopper to Greylock and Fitch. The road rises but this is an easy walk on an open road, suitable even for sneakers. It is also possible to drive, although there is a slight fee for driving to picnic at Stony Ledge. The afternoon is the best time to make the trip, because the sun strikes on the far ledges. An intriguing alternative from the same perch, however, is watching the sun rise over the highest peak in Massachusetts.

Other walks include a good bit of up-and-down, and so require stout shoes. A short but rugged trail departs across from the contact station, up a former road and then right, up and along a sidehill, then steeply down, less than a mi. in total, to the foot of March Cataract. Although a good flow of water tumbles down at all seasons, the walk is especially recommended in high water, when you will be well wetted before you stand on the midstream rocks — if you can — gazing up the gleaming wet stone face. It is dangerous to make this trip in the winter, because the trail cuts uncertainly along the sidehill, but it is a thrill to hear the water plunging beneath the ice. Note: this trail is less worn than most in the reservation and therefore harder to follow.

Departing Sperry Rd. on the same side as the contact station but a few hundred feet farther in, the Deer Hill Trail follows Roaring Brook, sharing the Roaring Brook Trail at first but turning left after 200 yds., passing Deer Hill Falls (1 mi.), and starting fairly steeply up, past a reconstructed lean-to, and coming out on the carriage road. Turn left to arrive at Sperry Rd. and left again to return to the contact station (2.25 mi.) If you don't turn on Sperry Rd., you will come out on the Hopper trail above the campground.

MOUNT PROSPECT FROM NOTCH ROAD

1 mile (30 minutes)

Climbing from the valley to the peak of Prospect is the steepest hike around (it begins partway along the Money Brook Trail, which in turn begins at the same point as the Hopper Trail). It is possible to get the same view, however, by driving up Notch Rd. 3 mi. from the gate to the AT crossing at the stand of tall spruce trees. There is an obvious parking area beyond and a big sign. Follow the white blazes down and then up. Where the AT meets the Prospect Trail, on the ridge (.5 mi.), an opening gives a fine view of Williamstown and especially the Galusha Farm, with cleared fields below you.

HIKES

CHESHIRE HARBOR TRAIL

6.6 miles (2.5 hours)

Road approaches

At the statue of former President McKinley in front of the library in Adams turn W. off Rte. 8 onto Maple St. At .4 mi. turn left on West Rd.; .5 mi. later, right on W. Mountain Rd. at sign for Mt. Greylock Greenhouses. The road ends at a turnaround, the site of a former farmhouse, after 1.6 mi. Most of the land may soon be subject to Greylock Center development, but the trailhead will remain open.

Camping

Peck's Brook shelter, a three-sided, Adirondack lean-to, is attained by a separate, 1-mi. trail that departs from the junction of Rockwell, Notch, and Summit roads. Bascom Lodge, at the summit, has limited accommodations (reservations required) as well as food. It is run by the AMC. All summit buildings are closed from late October until Memorial Day, but some protection may be found at the Thunderbolt Ski Shelter, with fireplace, on the AT just below the summit parking lot, to the north of the War Memorial Tower.

CHESHIRE HARBOR TRAIL

Mt. Greylock is very close to its east side approaches, although the summit is more of a haul than it looks as you stand on the old field at the end of the open section of W. Mountain Rd. Cheshire Harbor Trail is the shortest and easiest of the hiking routes to the summit, not only because of its directness but because it begins at a good elevation. It rises from 1,800 ft. to 3,491 ft. It is also heaviest traveled. Every Columbus Day, hundreds climb this route during the Greylock Ramble, sponsored by the Adams Chamber of Commerce. The trail has been badly eroded, mostly due to off-road vehicles, which have now been banned here (except for snowmobiles). Cheshire Harbor is the community in the town of Cheshire where the trail actually starts, about a mi. SE of where you start.

The unblazed trail leaves as a woods road, heading from the SW corner of the field. Old walls mark the site. Almost immediately the portion of the trail rising from Cheshire Harbor enters left. Riveted drainage pipes and barbed wire hark back to the time when this road served active farms.

At 11 min. you come to the first switchback and, in 3 more min., to the second, where a trail enters left (ignore it). Soon, depending on the condition of the foliage, you see the summit, with its tower, rising over Peck's Brook ravine. At 17 min. you round the third switchback and, 4 min. later, the junction with Old Adams Rd. makes the fourth. Old Adams Rd. follows more or less at this contour to the base of Jones' Nose, crossing the AT, which rises from the south. It was a stage route joining Adams and New Ashford; a farmhouse (no longer standing) at Jones' Nose served as a stop. Apparently the place was named for the profile of the farmer.

You bear right, staying on the Cheshire Harbor Trail, however, continuing up the moderate grade that characterizes this entire trail. The trail has been blazed blue or orange from time to time, although blazes are not needed. As you rise, the trail erosion diminishes. The northern hardwoods through which you pass are severely stressed, the effect of atmospheric pollution. Scientists have designated plots in the area to study the decline of high altitude forests in New England. The results to date are disturbing. You see many dead birch, beech, and maple. The ledges (left) rise to the ridge that connects Greylock with the next peak south, Saddleball.

At 54 min. you cross Peck's Brook. Soon a snowmobile trail, known as the Super Highway, drops right to the Gould Farm. Continue on to Rockwell Rd., an hour from the car. At this point you join the AT, following its white blazes to the summit. The next stretch parallels the road but is in the woods — which are, suddenly, the boreal, high elevation forest of balsam firs and bogs, which the trail crosses on bog bridges. The unnamed pond on the left was dug out of a wet spot by the CCC to serve as a water supply for Bascom Lodge.

At the 3-way road junction (1:08), follow straight ahead, back into the woods. The trail to Peck's Brook Shelter departs across the road, right. You follow the AT, with the old water pipe from the pumphouse on the pond; now the lodge has a drilled well. The next sound you hear may well be the wind in the guy wires of the television and radio broadcast tower, which you pass at 1:14. In 3 more min. you pass through the break in the stone walls and come to the War Memorial itself. For those who do not suffer from vertigo, the 92-ft. climb up stairs to the lookout is worthwhile, extending your view. It is also worthwhile to tour the summit on ground level, especially looking over the eastern side, directly down to the town of Adams — and, considerably nearer, Greylock Glen.

Remember to start down by the broadcast tower. The road crossings can be confusing, too. Cross the first, staying on the AT. After the second crossing, the AT continues straight (S.) while the Cheshire Harbor Trail bears left. The trip down takes just about the same time as up.

Since the summit is the focus of 43 miles of trails in the Greylock Reservation, numerous variations on this basic, east side climb are possible. If you can get someone to serve as chauffeur, an east to west hike across the ridge could begin on the Cheshire Harbor Trail and end on the Hopper Trail. Or, with the aid of a Berkshire Regional Transportation Authority bus from No. Adams to Cheshire, an east to north climb would link the Cheshire Harbor Trail with the Bellows Pipe Trail. (Hopper and Bellows Pipe trails are described farther on.) A loop, eschewing the summit, begins on Cheshire Harbor Trail, follows S. on the AT over Saddleball and past the Bassett Brook Campsite to Old Adams Rd. Follow left (N.) 1.5 mi. on Old Adams Rd. until it joins the Cheshire Harbor Trail again (about 15 mi.). Cheshire Harbor Trail and Old Adams Rd. are skiable with deep snow cover.

BELLOWS PIPE TRAIL

4.0 miles (1.5 hours) one way

Road approaches

Turn S. on Notch Rd., off Rte. 2 between Harriman-West Airport and the turn that leads to downtown No. Adams. The road climbs through a residential area and woods, turning sharply left at Mt. Williams Reservoir. After 2.4 mi. from Rte. 2, park along Notch Rd. before it turns right to enter the Mt. Greylock State Reservation; the road by Notch Reservoir comes in from the left. Do not park in such a way as to interfere with the private home at the corner. Bellows Pipe Trail is the gravel road straight ahead. (You can reach the same point via Reservoir Rd., also from No. Adams, or by Pattison Rd., the continuation of Luce Rd. in Williamstown.)

Camping

You pass a lean-to, a ski shelter, and Bascom Lodge on this hike. The lean-to is a bit more than halfway in time, where the Bellows Pipe Ski Trail meets the Bellows Pipe (hiking) Trail. It faces south. The ski shelter is next to the parking lot at the summit, and therefore inclined to be trashy regardless of how rigorously it is cleaned. With a large fireplace in the middle and open sides, it is meant for day use but is available at night for emergencies in the winter. Bascom Lodge stands firmly on the summit, a warm and cheery destination in summer and early fall.

BELLOWS PIPE TRAIL

Although this trail is too steep for a comfortable descent (see end of description for alternatives), it is hard to think of a better place to be under certain conditions than climbing the Bellows Pipe. One set of conditions is a sunny day on light, powdery snow — on skis. Another is a warm morning, as the fog burns off in the valley, perhaps in late May, when the ephemeral flowers are blossoming and all the brooks are running high. The sun bursts yellow through the trees, suddenly creating shadows where there had been none and picking out the dew on the shrubbery.

You are starting at 1,304 ft. in elevation and climbing to 3,491. In places, particularly on the Bellows Pipe Ski Trail, the going is quite steep. As you cross the chain on the road, it's clear you're on No. Adams watershed property, which protects Notch Reservoir, an impoundment of the brook that cut the valley you climb. There are no blazes on city land, which extends to the Notch. The large sugar maples beside the gravel road have been there many generations; the pines were planted as a way of having trees beside a reservoir that would not fill the water with leaves. You pass several cellar holes and old walls you probably won't notice if the foliage is out. But you may notice the road was uncommonly well made: edged with stone, built with a crown, ditched on the sides. In places it appears to have been cobbled.

For this and many other man-made features of the route, credit Jeremiah Wilber and his descendants, who cut a spacious and productive farm out of the wilderness of this mountain about 1800, built the first road to the summit, grew hay, boiled off enormous quantities of maple syrup, grazed his cattle, killed marauding wolves and bears, built three mills and raised a dozen children by two wives.

Yours is the route Henry David Thoreau took in 1844, when he heeded Hawthorne's and Emerson's advice to visit Greylock. (Emerson called it "a serious mountain.") At one of these homes, now a cellar hole, Thoreau stopped to converse with a lady who was combing her long tresses. You can read about it in *A Week on the Concord and Merrimack Rivers*. He spent the night in a wooden tower on the summit. When he awoke, the clouds had closed in below him, and he found himself "in a country such as we might see in dreams, with all the delights of paradise."

In 10 min. you come to a yarding area used for timber cutting, but continue straight on the unblazed trail. The going gets a bit steeper. Soon, through breaks in the foliage, you can see the ridge of Ragged Mtn. (which rises 2,451 ft.) to the east, over Notch Brook valley. The next landmark, at 31 min., is a bridge. This area is called Bellows Pipe, a name that Thoreau used. The name presumably derives from the fact that wind rushes through the notch just as air rushes through the pipe at the end of a bellows.

Having crossed a dozen or more tributaries, you finally cross the main stem of Notch Brook at 40 min. and after a short, very steep eroded section, are in the notch (2,197 ft. in elevation) cleared not long ago as an orchard. At the site of informal camping under spruces at the left, a marked trail follows the wall up to the cliffs on Ragged. Thoreau may have climbed up there to check his bearings before his final bushwack to the summit. Now that you are on state land, look for orange and blue blazes that lead to the summit.

Follow a level section, looking down into Adams. At 50 min. turn right on the blazed trail (the original road continues down to become Gould Rd. in Adams; see under alternate ways home). The shelter is on your right, almost immediately. You are now on the Bellows Pipe Ski Trail, cut by the CCCs in the 1930s, as you will recognize from the series of steep sharp switchbacks. At 1:02 do not take the unmarked trail straight ahead, which leads to the Thunderbolt. Instead, follow right, on a section that is a real workout if you are on skis. As a matter of fact, it's a workout on foot.

The trees are becoming lower and more scraggly on the steep eastern face — more beech and birch, somewhat stunted. After 5 switchbacks and testing ascents, you come out at 1:17 on the white-blazed AT, heading S. to the summit. Trees are often ice-covered on this stretch in the winter; if you catch them when the sun hits, the effect is of walking through a lighted chandelier. If a breeze is blowing, the branches clink together like cut glass, as well. Within a minute the AT joins the Thunderbolt Trail for the final assault. If you plan to descend this way, be sure to turn around at this point to check the lay of the land, which can be confusing on the way back. As the Indians said, "every trail is two trails, one going and one coming." Soon a blue blazed trail heads right, crossing nearby Notch Rd. to Robinson's Point. You continue on the steep Thunderbolt to cross Summit Rd. (1:26). The ski shelter the CCC built at the head of the Thunderbolt is right. You skirt the parking lot and arrive at the memorial tower at 1:30.

Remember, if you decide to return by this route, that you start on the AT N., by the parking lot. The AT S. takes off by the TV tower only partway around the compass. But the Bellows Pipe Ski Trail is too steep to be a pleasant descent, so choose a different way home. In the winter, ski down Notch Rd. to your car. Leave on Summit Rd. and turn right at the first intersection. You don't want to walk down a road with traffic in the summer, however, so you need to arrange a 2-car hike, with someone meeting you at the summit or at the base of another one of the trails described here. Cheshire Harbor, Hopper, and Roaring Brook are good trails down as well as up. A long alternative would be to make a loop by descending the Thunderbolt, again very steep, or the Gould Trail (a snowmobile trail across private property) to West Rd. to Notch Rd. in Adams (different from the 2 other Notch roads you've been on), which soon degenerates to a 4-wheel vehicle road and meets Reservoir Rd. at Notch Reservoir. That would add 16 mi. to your trip, for a total of 20. In effect, you would make a loop around Ragged; a shorter version would leave out the summit by following straight to Gould Rd. at the Notch.

THE HOPPER TRAIL

8 miles (3.5 hours)

Road approaches

Beginning at Field Park in Williamstown, follow Rte. 2 E. to Green River Rd. (.5 mi.). Turn right. Hopper Rd. turns left at Mt. Hope Park (2.5 mi.). Follow Hopper Rd. along the brook, past Bressett Rd., until it swings left (straight ahead is Potter Rd.) beyond some open fields. It turns to gravel, ending at a state parking area before the barn and farmhouse (2.75 mi.).

Camping

As well as Bascom Lodge at the summit, on this route you hike through Sperry Rd. Campground, with 34 tent and 5 group sites, including 2 three-sided shelters. No showers, no flush toilets, no hookups. The state collects a small fee in season for overnight parking, picnicking, or camping. The Deer Hill shelter, reconstructed by an Eagle Scout and his father, is within .5 mi. of the campground. Please note that the Hopper itself is classified as a low impact area: No fires, camping, or vehicles permitted, except for tent camping at the Haley field, at the beginning of the Money Brook Trail. The Sperry Rd. Campground is also convenient for the Stony Ledge and Roaring Brook Trails.

THE HOPPER TRAIL

This is the classic Greylock hike, from 1,096 ft. to the summit, 3,491 ft., on a historic trail, through the deeply eroded "grain hopper" that marks the western side of the Greylock massif. Hopper Rd. didn't originally end at the gate; instead, it passed between the stone walls you walk between and then forded Money Brook, continuing up the far side into the inner Hopper. The route you are following was originally laid out by Almond Harrison, who pioneered a farm at the campground site about 1800. President Edward Dorr Griffin dismissed his Williams College students from class on a May day in 1830 to improve this road and extend it to the summit, where they built the first tower. At the time, the summit was tree-covered, so the tower was the only alternative to shinnying up the stunted fir trees for a view. Later the CCC built its camp where Harrison's farm had been; still later the state developed its campgrounds in the same spot, as the spruces grew into the once-open fields.

Be sure to close the gate at the trailhead. Pass through the state vehicle gate. No dogs allowed. Stroll down the road between the hayfields, on which cows were recently pastured. Leave the old road, which continues as Money Brook Trail, at the sign (8 min.) for Hopper Trail, bearing right following the blue blazes to the edge of the upper field. There the trail plunges into the woods. For the next quarter mi. or so the trail has been carefully engineered to make it as dry as possible.

This steady, no nonsense rise, cut into the sidehill, was the first leg of the Berkshires-to-the-Cape Bridle Trail, which wandered across the Commonwealth in the later 19th century. The large birch trees seem to have reached the ends of their lives, as beech and maple crowd them out. At 34 min., the Money Brook cut-off drops into the valley. You can probably hear the song of Money Brook, floating from the floor. Just shy of an hour you reach Sperry Rd. and the campground. Turn left and, in 2 min., left again, across from the contact station, as the Hopper Trail, still blazed blue, leaves the road.

This climb (from here on identical to that described in the Stony Ledge hike) is fairly steep and worn, along the upper reach of Roaring Brook. You pass a lovely brook the CCCs developed as a water source when they had their camp at Sperry Rd. Turn left on the Deer Hill Trail, which was once a carriage road (1:15). This is relatively level and stone-covered, as erosion has removed the thin soil. Where the Overlook Trail exits (1:27), your trail turns steeper. Large trees are less frequent at the higher elevation, giving way to more shrubbery. Nick a corner of Rockwell Rd., at a spring, but stick to the woods, which soon turn to spruce. A new section of trail avoids coming out on the road again. From here to the summit, follow the white blazes. You cross swampy areas on foot bridges. At 1:35 you pass the pond, no longer used, dug to serve as a water supply for Bascom Lodge. Follow the AT across the road intersection a min. later. Study these road crossings so that you will know what to do on the return trip.

Climb steeply, through fir and spruce, crossing the old water line, for 8 min. until you reach the broadcast tower and 2 more min. to the Memorial Tower (1:46).

For the return, the broadcast tower is the landmark for the proper direction to depart the summit on the AT. At 10 min. you cross the intersection, still on the AT, even though the "Adams" sign may momentarily confuse you. You pass the pond. Six more min. take you to the next road crossing where, instead of following the AT, you turn right, down the road and back into the woods at the "Hopper" sign. Continue on the Deer Hill Trail until the Hopper Trail exits, right, at a brook (35 min.). After you turn right on Sperry Rd., look for the Hopper Trail angling off to the right. The return trip takes 1:30, for a total travel time of 3:17.

You needn't return the way you came, of course. The most obvious circuit — up the Hopper trail and down Money Brook — is lengthy if you include the summit: 11 mi., via the AT over Mt. Williams to Tall Spruces. After you cross Notch Rd., take a left towards the shelter on the Money Brook Trail. You can save more than a mi. by cutting off the AT prior to Mt. Williams and hiking down the road .5 mi. to the cutoff for the Money Brook Trail. Shorter still would be to omit the summit of Greylock — all right to do after you've hit the summit a few times. Take the Hopper Trail to the Overlook Trail. Follow the Overlook Trail until it meets Notch Rd. Take Notch Rd. 100 yds. N.

to the cutoff to the AT on top of the ridge, and continue as described above. This route runs about 8 mi. A more attractive, although steep, shorter (6.5 mi.) hike links Money Brook and Prospect Trails.

STONY LEDGE AND ROARING BROOK TRAILS

9.0 miles (3.75 hours)

Road approaches

Beginning at Field Park in Williamstown, drive S. on Rte. 7, 5.5 mi. to Roaring Brook Rd., left just before the Massachusetts Department of Public Works garage; alternately, coming from the S., after entering Williamstown, turn right immediately beyond the garage. Drive 1 mi. up the gravel road until you see the sign indicating the private Mt. Greylock Ski Club. Use the parking area large enough for 3 or 4 cars just downstream from the sign; in the unlikely event that area is filled, you will have pull over nearer Rte. 7.

Camping

See description under Hopper Trail.

STONY LEDGE TRAIL

You can call this loop Stony Ledge for the first eminence, with its spectacular view of the Hopper, but you actually hike on several other trails: Hopper, Appalachian, and Roaring Brook, for instance. You rise from a deep valley, through the plateau that hosts a campground, to the summit, and back down through a hemlock forest. Both ascent and descent have steep sections. This hike is the most logical one if your goal is to sit on the edge of the abyss at Stony Ledge.

The trailhead is streamside, across from the ski club sign. You begin on a well-established old woods road, blazed blue for the most part, although some of previous white blazes persist. You cross Roaring Brook on a bridge, beyond the old wagon ford. You climb, passing a trail that rises into the fields, left. After 10 min. you drop down to the brook again and cross it on a log bridge. The old trail, exiting right, rises to the ski club. At 13 min. you cross a plank bridge. Just beyond, bear left on Stony Ledge rather than straight on Roaring Brook, on which you will return.

The sign indicates the wide, grassy trail to be an "intermediate ski trail," which refers to downhill skiing. Nordic skiing here is "advanced." Although you can see how the CCCs laid it out wide enough to enable some maneuvering, it hasn't been maintained for skiing.

Soon the trail picks up an old road, which it follows most of the rest of the way. From time to time you will see the telltale charcoal bits indicating charcoal burning sites. The product was used to smelt iron ore until the late 19th century when the Bessemer process came in. At 30 min. the trail begins to bear left and climb sharply, which it continues to do, with a branch of Roaring Brook left, to the ridge you soon will see to the right.

You arrive at Sperry Rd. at 53 min. Walk straight ahead to the gravel turnaround. Sit and absorb the summit and ridge across the chasm. The morning is not as good a time as evening because of shadows, but on the wall opposite you can see dark stands of red spruce, some nearly 200 years old, probably the oldest stands in the Commonwealth. You can also see March Cataract, to the southeast. It won't be prominent when late summer reduces the water flow, however.

Walk down the road about a mi., between azaleas and berry bushes into the camping area. You can easily see why Sperry Rd. is regarded as the best laid out campground around. Autos stay by the road; campers walk in 50 or 75 ft. to the sites, which are separated from one another for privacy. At 1:10 the Hopper Trail enters the road from the left. You see the Roaring Brook Trail entrance, right. At 1:13 the Hopper Trail exits, with you, to the left, across from the contact station.

Climb fairly steeply on a well-worn path, still blazed blue, which joins Deer Hill Trail (actually a carriage road), on which you turn left at 1:25. The path is relatively level until the Overlook Trail exits, left (1:37). You are surrounded by the big leaves of the hobble bush, known as the woodsman's toilet paper. You come out on a corner of Rockwell Rd. but stay to the woods, which soon turn to spruce. A new section of trail avoids coming out on the road again. You cross bridges over swamp. At 1:45 you pass the pond the CCC dug, no longer used. Follow the AT across the road intersection a min. later. Study the layout of these road crossings for the way back.

Eight min. later you climb steeply to the broadcast tower and 2 min. later (1:56), the War Memorial Tower. Cross to the E. side, drop over the edge a bit, and look down on the cleared fields and ponds of Greylock Glen. Look close, don't they?

The broadcast tower is your landmark for the proper direction to depart the summit on the AT. At 10 min. you cross the intersection, on the AT, even though the "Adams" sign may momentarily confuse you. You pass the pond. At 10:16, the next road crossing, instead of following the AT, bear right. Turn off the Deer Hill Trail, right, at 35 min., following the brook, more or less, to the campground.

In 42 min. from the summit (2:38), turn right on Sperry Rd. and shortly left, where the sign says "Roaring Brook Trail," blazed blue (occasionally white), across a bridge, and right along the brook. The Circular Trail leaves left in 5 min., but you cross the bridge; just beyond the bridge the Deer Hill Trail leaves left. Stay with Roaring Brook. You pass through hobble bush, black raspberries, beech, and maple. You descend steadily through hemlock, aware of a brook on each side. The descent becomes steep.

Gradually the two brook branches come closer, as you descend, until you must cross the smaller (3:16). You are at the junction with Stony Ledge Trail. After crossing the bridge and attaining some height, look down into the scenic, rocky gorge, where you can see the remains of a mill run. Farther downstream, in the day lilies, is the cellar hole for the mill. At 1:35 from the summit or 3:31 round trip you will be back at your starting point.

Skiers should do the loop by climbing Roaring Brook to Sperry Rd. and returning via Stony Ledge. Hikers go the opposite direction purely for the aesthetic satisfaction of coming out at the end of the climb on Stony Ledge. They might prefer the 3-mi. shorter version, however, omitting the summit. In season, the hike could be spiced up with a visit to March Cataract or Deer Hill falls. You can link all other Greylock trails to these 2, for 2-car variations on this hike.

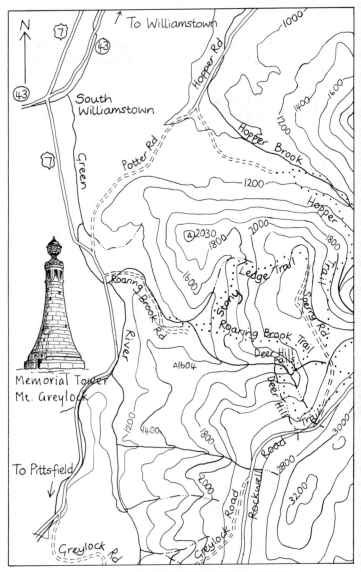

ADAMS: MT. GREYLOCK WALKS & HIKES

ADAMS: MT. GREYLOCK WALKS & HIKES

WILLIAMSTOWN

Soldiers at Fort Massachusetts, once located where the Price Chopper supermarket now resides on Rte. 2 in No. Adams, built the first homes in the township west of the fort and held their first Proprietors' Meeting there in 1753. Then a flare-up of the French and Indian War drove them out; of the original residents only Benjamin Simonds returned, with a wife, after having been in prison in Quebec. Their daughter, Rachael, was the first child of European stock born in the area. Simonds' River Bend Tavern still stands, run now as a bed and breakfast, on Simonds' Rd. (Rte. 7 north of town).

Still an active farming town, Williamstown is more famous for the college that has grown up with it. Ephraim Williams Jr. was a commander at the fort; on his way to battle at Lake George in 1755, he rewrote his will to establish a secondary school for the children of his command. Town and school were named for his generosity. The trustees converted his school into Williams College, which opened in 1793.

The college has attracted to the community the Clark Art Institute, with its ravishing collections of French Impressionists and 19th-century American artists and sculptors, and the Williamstown Theatre Festival, busy all summer with myriad main stage and experimental productions, readings, and cabarets. Both have been singled out by tough critics as the best of their kinds in the United States.

So, should the weather turn sour, despair not. The Clark (open even on Monday in the summer) provides an eyeful that can last all day. Other undercover destinations: the Williams College Museum of Art, the Hopkins Forest Farm Museum, the Chapin Rare Books Library, and the planetarium show at the Old Hopkins Observatory (reservations required). As well as shopping on Spring and Water streets, visitors may take tours of the Williams College campus, which originate at the admission office, Main St.

WALK

STONE HILL

1.5 miles (1 hour)

For Williamstown's favorite walk, drive S. on South St., beginning at Field Park, across from the Williams Inn. At a half mi., turn right into the Clark Art Institute. Drive under the bridge and turn left for the far side of the parking lot, behind the main building.

This leisurely stroll will take you from the Clark parking lot, 750 ft. in elevation, on a meandering path through old-growth, northern hardwood forest, to a stone seat at 1,000 ft.; then down through open fields, with a striking view of downtown Williamstown and the surrounding hills, and back to the parking lot.

To find the trailhead, look for 2 small gravestones that mark the eternal resting place of dogs that belonged to a previous owner of the property, Dr. Vanderpool Adriance. Sterling and Francine Clark purchased his land and built the white marble building for their art collection. It was opened to the public in 1955. The darker building to the right was built as an addition to the institute in 1973. The trail and footbridge were built in 1985 to help celebrate the Clark Institute's 30th anniversary. The trail, with clear signs, passes through a variety of birch, beech, and maple stands, as well as some hemlock and pine, so that the stroller can compare and enjoy, working gradually uphill.

At about 15 min., note a signed trail that turns right to the open fields you will pass through later. You continue straight to the remains of the colonial Stone Hill Rd., which preceded Rte. 7 as the main north-south route in the county. The road has been improved as access to the town's water tank, buried under a field. Follow up the hill to the stone seat erected as a memorial to George Moritz Wahl, a professor of German at Williams College who was incorrectly suspected by some of being a German spy during World War I. He was accustomed to climbing to this spot in the evening to watch the sunset — in those days the fields were open. This monument was the town's apology and tribute.

This is the far point of the hike, but you might like to continue S. on the old road, to see how the hill got its name. If you look through the trees to your left, you will see the schist outcroppings. After returning, walk through the gate across from the seat, carefully closing it behind you because cows may be pasturing in the fields. (Cows are curious enough to look you over but are harmless.) Head down, following the open land as it swings right. Although the trail remains clear, it passes through a short stretch of forest, emerging at the head of a long, sloping field. Set your sights to the right of a clump of trees on the ridge ahead, dipping down and then rising to a view that includes the Clark, Main St. and college, the Dome in southern Vermont, East Mtn. (encompassing Pine Cobble and Eph's Lookout), the Hoosac Valley heading into No. Adams, the Hoosac Range beyond the city, and the Greylock Range. The ridge is the ideal picnic site on this trip. You can keep the view in sight as you wander down the field, looking for the stone gateposts at the lower left corner.

Follow across the next field, heading down the hill to the wooden gate. Note: you are now part of the view for museum-goers. Perhaps you are being compared to the pastoral subject of an old master. Act accordingly. You are passing through what was called a "haha" in the 18th century. This device enclosed stock by a ditch, although the fence that would have been visible at the bottom has been moved to the edge of the parking lot.

Picnic tables rest under the trees around the parking lot. In the summer months a cafe serves light lunches in the lobby of the newer building, if that fits your strolling plans. Longer walks are possible, although they cross private land not necessarily open to the public. The Taconic Golf Course, across South St., is open for cross-country skiing.

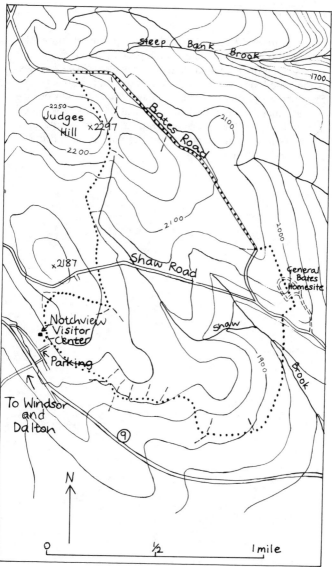

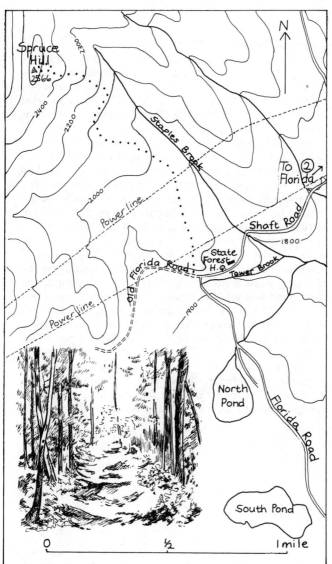

Spruce
Hill
△∴
2566

2200

2400

2200

2000

Staples Brook

To
Florida ②

Shaft Road

Power line

1800

State
Forest
H.Q.

Tower Brook

Old Florida Road

1900

Power line

North
Pond

Florida Road

South Pond

0 ½ 1 mile

FLORIDA & SAVOY: SPRUCE HILL

supported the considerable dwelling. The cellar stones were cut; where the house faced downhill are elaborate terraces, now overgrown, connected by steps. This site appears to have been a farm that by 1904 started taking in summer boarders. It was donated to the Florida-Savoy Land Trust in 1916 and thence to the state. George Busby, however, was granted the right to cross the property to the town road (Central Shaft Rd.) via the county road (Adams-Florida).

From here on, the trail rises more steeply. After 5 min. it crosses through a wall, apparently with a former road on the up side. Soon you reach the first of 2 steep but brief ascents over rocks. You come out on the outcroppings, looking east, after 45 min. You parked your car at 1,900 ft. in elevation; this summit rises to 2,566, the highest on the Hoosac plateau (except the tower on Borden Mtn.). The view down into the Hoosac Valley and up to the Greylock massif rewards your final burst of effort. The view south, over the Hoosac plateau, is no slouch, either. The trail continues on the summit to other cliffs, where the view of the Green Mtns. improves. These cliffs are an excellent vantage point to watch kettles of hawks cavort in the warm air rising from the valley during the fall migration. A short loop returns you to the Busby Trail.

What with taking it easy on the steep sections and examining the artifacts, it will take you about as long to get down as to climb. If you take the ski option, presumably you park them to climb the last few feet of rocks.

FLORIDA AND MONROE: TUNNEL AND TURBINE

Driving to the trailhead for Spruce Mtn. you pass 2 man-made points of particular interest. The first, in Florida, Massachusetts, is the eastern end of the Hoosac Tunnel. Look left as you cross the railroad tracks. On February 9, 1875, a steam engine first chugged from the Deerfield River Valley to the Hoosic River Valley, in No. Adams, through a 4.75-mi.-long tunnel, the longest in the world at the time, bored at a cost of 24 years, $15 million, and 195 lives. Discarding an idea dating back to 1825 to surmount the Hoosac Range by canal, those who wanted to join Boston and Albany by this northern route used the best available technology, drilling by hand and blasting with black powder through the rock. Two huge power drills, intended to do the work, both proved incapable; however, an air drill was successfully introduced in 1865. At the same time, George A. Mowbray tried a new explosive called nitroglycerin, a great improvement in blasting but dangerously unstable. A crazy, drunk assistant learned the lucky way that it could be frozen and carried safely. Freight trains still use the line, even though passenger service has long since faded from the northern Berkshire scene.

Florida was a boom town when the tunnel was under construction, especially the village known as Hoosac Tunnel, at the eastern end. Now you hardly know you are passing through a town. That anything more still exists than a few farms is probably because of the New England Power Company's Bear Swamp pumped storage hydroelectric project in the next town upriver and across the Franklin County line, Monroe. Although several hydroelectric units had existed in the valley previously, the Bear Swamp project was built in the 1970s. The Bear Swamp Visitors' Center, on River Rd. north of the tunnel, shows an interesting slide-tape on the history of the valley and a working exhibit of pumped storage. The local Massachusetts Electric Co. office can arrange a tour of the power plant. You drive across the dam and walk down a tunnel into the side of Rowe Mtn. for 690 ft. until you are in the powerhouse. Then you descend

5 stories, viewing control equipment and getting a look at the huge, twin pump-turbines that generate electricity during peak load periods as water is let out of the Upper Reservoir. The process is reversed, pumping from the Lower Reservoir 770 ft. up to the Upper Reservoir, during off-peak times. The penstock that carries the water is 17.5 ft. in diameter. Construction of the powerhouse involved removing 97,800 cubic yards of stone.

Road approaches

Go E. from Florida, above and east of No. Adams on what is known locally as the Trail (the Mohawk Trail, Rte. 2), take the next left after Whitcomb Summit; then the next right. You head down on a steep road to a T at River Rd. The river is the Deerfield. Go left at the T, continuing through the village of Hoosac Tunnel. Soon you pass the Bear Swamp Visitors' Center, right, where you might wish to stop. The parking area you want to find for the hike is on the left, .75 mi. beyond the visitors' center, 4.5 mi. from the Trail.

Camping

You will pass 3 lean-tos (three-sided) shelters, all of which are well maintained (by the state and power company), and numerous fireplaces and informal camping areas. A word of caution, though: all the shelters are within a couple miles of a road and show evidence of being sites for parties. Ideally, as well, shelters should be located a bit off the trail. Using these is like sleeping in the hall. Few services or accommodations are available in Hoosac Tunnel or the next town up, Monroe Bridge, so plan accordingly.

Do not confuse the Spruce Hill hike in Florida with this one on Spruce Mtn. in Monroe. Several other spruce hills and mountains exist in the area, for the obvious botanical reason.

HIKE

DUNBAR BROOK

9 miles (4 hours)

Spruce Mtn. in Monroe State Forest, Franklin County, is a pleasant hike, not too steep on the south side. There are fine vistas from wire cuts — that is, swaths opened for power lines — and three cliffs along the way. The mountain does not have a cleared summit. A short sidetrip, partway up, leads to Raycroft Lookout, for a view of the Deerfield Valley. Other links of this loop, all blazed blue, climb up the Dunbar Brook Valley and pass over former and present woods roads. The best is last: the truly scenic walk down Dunbar Brook Trail, beside the tumbling waters of the clear, mountain stream, through glades of enormous hemlock, which look as though the underbrush were swept out every day. The Commonwealth has declared the Dunbar Valley, like Alander Mtn. and the Hopper on Mt. Greylock, special Backcountry Areas.

This walk takes you through and near ancient and undisturbed stands of trees, some individuals more than 250 years old. Some are large, but conditions more than age determine size.

The Dunbar picnic area, maintained by New England Power Co., is on the east side of River Rd. Your trailhead, a smaller parking lot, is directly across from it. Start up to the power line, at the SW corner of the lot. Above the dam, the trail detaches itself from the jeep road and drops towards the brook, which it follows under spreading hemlock. Look for the blue blazes. Solomon's seal, trilliums, and other spring ephemerals flower in profusion, so that in late May it is impossible to avoid stepping on their beautiful blossoms. After 12 min. the trail turns left at a bench and fireplace, following close to the river for 4 min. You turn up the hill at the trail junction just before the bridge — which you will cross on your return.

For the next 15 min. you zigzag up the Dunbar Brook Valley wall. A stone cairn is the sign you are almost at the first shelter; 5 more min. takes you to Raycroft Extension, a dirt road with large puddles. This is prime mosquito and blackfly land; wear your favorite bug repellent. Turn right, following the blue dots. In 7 min. you turn left on a former woods road, somewhat grown in. At 50 min. from departure you pass the second shelter of the outing, turning sharp right. Straight ahead is deceptively like a path, but actually an intermittent brook bed.

In 55 min. you pass under a power line you will cross 3 more times. If the trail has not been bushed recently, it may be hard to spot the opening directly across the cleared area. You could follow the line, left, as a short cut, but aren't you in this to hike? The route is steep and rocky, as well. Ignore extraneous woods roads. Follow the blazes. An hr. from the parking lot, you meet South Rd. As a check, turning left you should see a cement boundary marker, right. Choices: You can turn right for the quickest way to Dunbar Brook; you can turn left and, in 7 min., right, for a 1 hr., 20 min. jaunt on Spruce Hill; or you can turn left and left again for a 37 min. (times 2) visit to Raycroft lookout tower.

The instructions for Spruce Hill follow. In 7 min. you will cross under those familiar wires, which alert you that you will soon turn. In 4 more min., at an intersection of gravel roads, follow the trail, still blazed blue, right. (Turn left for the lookout.)

Shortly you pass under those wires, again: This time the cut gives you a nice view of the church spire in Florida. You climb moderately to a plateau, through spruce, oak, and maple, over quartzite outcroppings. In 20 min. you come to a view, left, over a cliff, of the Hoosac peneplain, the truncated remains of a mountain range. You are in a beech forest. You may think you've reached the summit when the trail begins to descend; but like the boat *Mary Ellen Carter*, it rises again, for about 20 more min., to the summit (2,751 ft. in elevation; you began at about 1,100 ft.). Cliffs to the left show you a view south similar to one you've seen before.

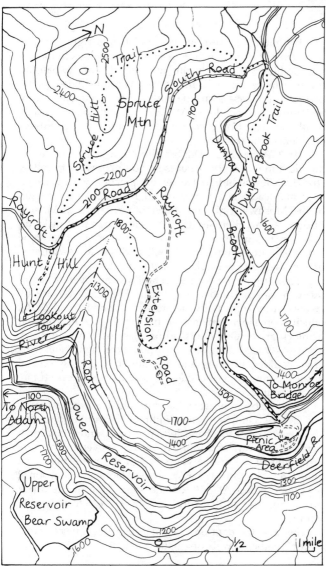

FLORIDA & MONROE: DUNBAR BROOK

Beginning its descent, the trail bends right. At 1:58 you arrive at a trail junction in a bog; stay right, still following the blue. The trail begins to descend sharply, pausing for one more outlook, this time over the hydroelectric project. You pass some beautiful ash specimens before reclaiming the hemlock. At 2:20, turn left on that same South Rd. you trod before. Look left for some enormous boulders in the woods.

At 2:23 you cross Dunbar Brook on a wooden, automobile bridge. To orient yourself, you may want to follow straight a few hundred feet to the junction with a paved road that leads, as a section called Tilda Rd., from the top of the Mohawk Trail and under other names to Monroe Bridge — an alternate driving route. Your trail picks up downstream, just on the north side of the bridge, past some old mill foundations. The brook beckons for swimming or sunning; less public places lie down below.

Thus begins the longest as well as the loveliest leg of the trip, down Dunbar to the car. The trail you are on swings away from the water to join a woods road (2:26), which soon tapers down to a trail through a magnificent hemlock grove. One thousand needles cushion your every tread. As you descend to the brook, bear right before the large boulder; then zig and zag down. You cross several brooks joining from the side . . . and then, yes, once more the wire cut (2:55).

And just 6 min. later, the third shelter, where a large brook joins Dunbar, stands right in the trail. Of several choices, you want to bend left. You pass, under continual hemlocks, several informal fireplaces. Seven more min. bring you to the bridge you saw but did not cross 3 hrs. ago. Cross it now. It hangs across Dunbar Brook on 2 telephone poles. At 3:10, on the south side of the brook now, you come to that turn; 10 min. more returns you to your car.

Because the dam on Dunbar Brook has a fence across it, don't bother to walk down the trail to it.

WALKS FOR THE BLIND
AND DISABLED
by Robert J. Redington

Robert J. Redington lost his sight in 1982. Previously an ardent Berkshire hiker, he had an important role in establishing the southern end of the Taconic Skyline Trail (see Long Hikes*). Since then he has been working to help blind people enjoy the out-of-doors. Redington describes the following trails for the use of sighted people in assisting the blind to walk in the woods. He suggests that generally the sighted person walk beside the visually handicapped person, explaining any obstacles and also describing the wildlife and views. Where the trail is narrower, the sighted person should walk in front, holding one end of a stick or rope that the blind person also holds with a hand on the same side. A walking stick for the blind person can also be fun and useful. Redington chose relatively smooth trails. The Commonwealth of Massachusetts wishes to cooperate by designating appropriate trails for the blind. In addition, the state has created a wheelchair accessible path, known as Tranquility Trail, at Pittsfield State Forest (for directions see Pittsfield, this section). Bob Redington graciously allowed us to edit his descriptions for this book.*

SOUTH COUNTY

GREAT BARRINGTON AND MONTEREY

WALKS

BEARTOWN STATE FOREST, BENEDICT POND

l.5 miles or more

Road approach

Coming down Rte. 7 from Stockbridge, turn left just beyond the high school onto Monument Valley Rd. Follow it to Stony Brook Rd., where you turn left. Stony Brook becomes Blue Hill Rd. Continue to Beartown State Forest entrance, left. The pond is uphill into the woods. Parking is provided. From Gt. Barrington, go east on Rte. 23 to Blue Hill Rd. in Monterey, turn left, continue past state forest headquarters to the entrance road to the pond.

BENEDICT POND

Beautiful Benedict Pond lies in Beartown State Forest. It is surrounded by woods where mountain laurel bloom in late June and early July. Canada geese are on the pond in the summer. Alternative hiking routes around the pond can be taken. One, which is nearer the shore with more views of the pond, is the Pond Loop Trail, marked by triangular blue painted blazes and 1.5 mi. long. The other route, which is longer and easier walking, follows a road, a woods road (a route with a natural surface and wide enough for a four-wheel vehicle), and a cross-country ski trail. A combination of the 2 routes can also be followed.

Benedict Pond is the recreation center of Beartown State Forest, with hiking, picnicking, camping, swimming, and, if you bring your own boat — or rent a boat from the concessionaire — canoeing, rowing, and fishing (no motors). A day-use fee is charged per car during the Memorial Day weekend to Labor Day season, but not for a handicapped person suitably identified.

POND LOOP TRAIL

This trail is rough in places, with rocks and roots under foot and a few steep steps. There are also log bridges and walkways along the trail. These sections call for close guidance by the sighted guide. Hiking is mostly single file along the trail, so the blind hiker and guide should use a guiding stick or rope tether.

The trail starts from the parking area at the Pond Loop Trail sign and blue blaze. Follow it E. along the south side of the pond, passing viewpoints at the edge of the pond a few paces to the left of the trail.

The Loop Trail turns left onto the white-blazed Appalachian Trail (AT), which it follows at the eastern end of the pond. At a point here you can go left a short distance to a fine vantage point at the edge of the pond.

The trail turns left again on a wood road, and in a few yds. the AT goes right while the Loop Trail continues ahead on the wood road, now on the east side of the pond. Next, the trail turns left from the wood road at the sign and follows the northeast and north sides of the pond. Finally, the trail turns down the west side of the pond, passing through the campground and ending at a trail sign at the shore of the pond a few yds. before the dam at the pond's outlet. There are picnic tables here and a swimming beach nearby.

To complete the circuit back to the parking area, cross on the dam, and go through the picnic area on the wooded knoll to the parking area.

THE LONGER CIRCUIT ROUTE

This route is a mile or so longer than the Loop Trail. It provides smoother walking and is mostly wide enough to permit the blind hiker to walk beside the guide. From the same parking area, take the paved road, which is blocked by a metal gate and has a sign saying, "To the Appalachian Trail," and follow it eastward parallel to the Loop Trail on the south side of the pond. After the AT crosses the road, the pavement ends at a triangular Y junction, where you take the left fork onto the previously mentioned wood road. Soon the combined AT-Pond Loop Trail enters the wood road from the left. Follow the wood road northward on the eastern side of the pond, passing the point where the Loop Trail turns away from it. In another half mi., a few yds. before the wood road reaches the paved Beartown Rd., turn left onto the cross-country ski trail marked by triangular red blazes. Follow this ski trail SW to the camping area where it crosses the Loop Trail. Turn right on the Loop Trail for the short distance to its end near the dam.

CENTRAL COUNTY

BECKET

NATURE TRAILS

OCTOBER MOUNTAIN STATE FOREST, FINERTY POND

4 miles

Road approaches

From Lee go left (N.) off Rte. 20 on Becket Rd., which soon becomes Tyne Rd. as it enters Becket from Lee. A half-mile from the junction with Rte. 20, turn left into a wood road and park immediately on the right.

FINERTY POND

Hike north for about a mi. on the woods road gravel, which is easy walking with a gradual ascent, and reach a junction with a left and right fork. Take the right fork, an old CCC road made with a cobblestone base. There are 2 rough rocky sections along it, but the route continues to be relatively level. After less than a mi. on this woods road the AT, with white painted blazes, crosses it. Turn left on the AT, which descends towards nearby Finerty Pond. Soon reach a junction where the AT turns left and an unmarked trail goes right. Continue straight ahead on a faint trail a short distance to the edge of the pond and go a few yds. to the right to a large log at the edge of the pond, which is good for several people to sit on. Sighted persons have a good view of the attractive pond from here.

Return to the starting point, retracing your steps over the same route. If you wish to walk farther, when you reach the AT from the edge of the pond, turn left on the un-marked trail and follow it along the southeast side of the pond to the dam at the pond's outlet. There are views over the pond along here. Then retrace your steps. The dam can also be reached by continuing a short way along the woods road beyond the AT crossing, and descending left to the aforementioned unmarked trail to follow it right to the dam.

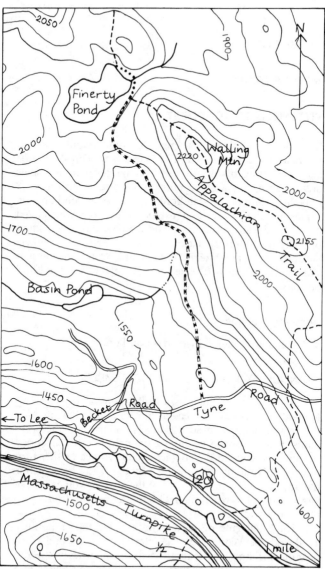

OCTOBER MTN. STATE FOREST: FINERTY POND

PITTSFIELD

NATURE TRAILS

PITTSFIELD STATE FOREST

There are two self-guiding interpretive nature trails in the main recreational area of Pittsfield State Forest, an area also containing hiking, ski, and snowmobile trails, picnic areas, campsites, a swimming pond, and a ski jump. A notable feature of the state forest is the Berry Pond area on the crest of the Taconic Range, reached by a one-way, paved circuit road. Here there are splendid views, the largest stand of wild (Pinkster) azaleas in Massachusetts, the highest natural pond in the state (Berry Pond at 2,060 ft.), and another self-guiding nature trail especially rewarding for blind persons.

Road approaches

See directions under "Pittsfield, Berry Pond."

TRANQUILITY TRAIL AND WOODS RAMBLE

At the entrance there is a contact station where an attendant collects day-use fees from cars during the late May to early September season. There is no charge if the occupants of a car are to go hiking or include a handicapped person. Just beyond the contact station you can either turn left and drive to the parking area by the ski lodge, which is the access to the 2 nature trails of the area, or you can drive straight ahead to reach the HQ building and to drive up to the Berry Pond area.

The 2 self-guiding nature trails, called the Tranquility Trail and the Woods Ramble, start from the same place near the ski lodge. Each is about a half-mi. long, has numbered signposts along it and makes a loop, which you follow in a counterclockwise direction, keeping to the right where the loop starts. Each trail is wide enough for the blind person to walk beside the guide. The Tranquility Trail is paved, so it may be used by persons in wheelchairs and by those who walk with difficulty. The Woods Ramble Trail is rougher and climbs a way. There are blue painted blazes on part of the trail and on the Hawthorne Trail, which branches off it, so care should be taken to remain on the route with the numbered signposts, shown on the map contained in the Woods Ramble Trail leaflet.

The self-guiding leaflet for each trail, entitled "Nature's Secrets" in the case of the Tranquility Trail, has numbered paragraphs giving information regarding the plant life and other natural features near the corresponding numbered posts. Each leaflet contains information not provided in the other, and the Woods Ramble leaflet gives additional information of interest concerning the natural history and ecology of Pittsfield State Forest. The two leaflets, as well as the one for the nature trail near Berry Pond, may be obtained from the contact station. The sighted persons can help the blind feel plant life and other natural objects along the trail. If blind persons walking the Tranquility Trail prefer to listen to a recording of the information on the leaflet, they may obtain, at the HQ building, the necessary cassette player and tape.

An additional walk of a mi. or so to state forest recreational sites may be taken. Start off by walking along the paved road past the ski lodge for some distance. Then turn right on the gravel crossroad, and near its end turn left onto a trail that leads to the ski jump and the swimming pond, formed by a dam in Lulu Brook. You can then either retrace your steps or return via the paved road which passes the HQ building. The walk will also take you past picnic grounds and campsites. You can consult a state forest leaflet and map obtained from the contact station or the HQ building.

BERRY POND AREA

BERKSHIRE HILLS RAMBLE

During the non-snow season, usually mid-April through October, you can drive up the Berry Pond Circuit Rd., a one-way route which climbs 1,000 ft. to the crest of the range and descends again to the main recreational area. As you reach the crest, look for a broad trail going left from the road where there should be a sign, and where on the right there is a space for 2 or 3 cars to park. This is the beginning of the Berkshire Hills Ramble, an interesting, self-guiding nature trail with numbered signposts corresponding to numbered paragraphs on the trail's leaflet. The trail descends somewhat and makes a loop (followed in the clockwise direction), which passes the edge of Berry Pond, the distance ending back at the starting point about .75 mi. Blind persons can enjoy the fragrance of the ferns, balsam firs, and the azalea bushes when in blossom, and they can listen to the frogs in the pond.

Drive another .25 mi. or so along the road on the crest of the range, past the azalea stands, and park on the right where there is a fine panoramic view over New York State to the west. Then walk up the broad trail to the right of the parking area for a short climb to the top of Berry Hill, 2,200 ft. in elevation. Here there is a bushy growth and further views. Continue down the other side of the hill, following occasional white trail markers, to the paved road. Turn right to walk back along the road to the parking area. Alternatively, if you did not visit the nature trail on the drive up, you can go a few yds. along the road to reach that trail on the left. When you have finished the trail, you walk left on the road for the .25 mi. back to the parking area. The walk over Berry Hill and along the paved road, as well as on the nature trail, is the best way to view the azalea bushes when they are in bloom, usually during the first week in June.

If you continue walking along the road past the parking area, you will descend a short distance to Berry Pond on the left. Here an open grassy area gives access to the shore of the pond. You can then follow a broad trail marked with an occasional white painted blaze, which goes between the road and the pond and passes several campsites by the pond. Each one has a picnic table and fireplace. You can then walk back to the parking area and continue driving along the one-way road back down to the main recreational area of the state forest, where the road passes the ski lodge and the access to the 2 nature trails.

WASHINGTON

WALK

WARNER HILL / APPALACHIAN TRAIL

2 miles

Road approaches

Drive E. on Williams St. in Pittsfield, fork left on Kirchner, and make the long climb up the highland to where the AT crosses the road 3.1 mi. from the junction below. The trail crossing here is in Washington, where Kirchner becomes Blotz, although there is no sign indicating the name change. From the east one can reach the trailhead from Rte. 8 in Hinsdale, from where it is 1.4 mi. along the Blotz/Kirchner side road westward to the trailhead.

Park in the space, if empty, on the north side of Blotz Rd. where the white-blazed AT crosses the road.

WARNER HILL / APPALACHIAN TRAIL

Hike N. on the AT, the blind person using a guiding stick or rope tether with the sighted guides. Near the start of the hike pass several fragrant balsam fir trees and cross 2 muddy spots on stones, if possible. Gradually ascend Warner Hill, passing an extensive stand of red spruce trees and fragrant fern beds. After almost a mi., reach the summit of Warner Hill, at 2,050 ft. A short, narrow side trail loops right from the AT to go over the high point of Warner Hill. From this rocky summit there is a view of Pittsfield to the northwest, of the Taconic Range beyond, and of Mt. Greylock to the north. Trees have been cut down to open up this view.

Continue N. on the AT a short way down from the summit to an extensive stand of fragrant ferns. Before retracing your route to the trailhead, you may wish to hike farther N. on the trail, as it gradually descends Warner Hill.

From the trail crossing of Blotz, you may wish to hike another half-mile or so S. on the AT. This is pleasant, level walking, past some conifer trees, and you can turn back where the trail starts to climb. There are log walkways over wet places along this trail section.

NORTH COUNTY

ADAMS

MOUNT GREYLOCK STATE RESERVATION, MOUNT PROSPECT

Road approaches

See directions (and information about facilities) under "Adams and Mt. Greylock."

MOUNT PROSPECT

This excursion is recommended to last from morning into the afternoon, including lunch. It should be between Memorial Day weekend and mid-October. Generally, the walking is more difficult than on other recommended paths for the handicapped. There are 2 short, self-guiding nature trails in the Mt. Greylock State Reservation. One starts from the east end of the parking lot of the Visitors' Center on Rockwell Rd. as you begin your drive up the mountain, and the other is located on the mountain range above on the north side of Sperry in the public campground. If you wish to visit either trail, or both, ask at the Visitors' Center for the self-guiding leaflet for the trail. At the numbered stops along the trail, the sighted guide can read to the blind person the information in the leaflet concerning the plant life and other natural features at these locations.

After visiting the Greylock summit, drive back down to the fork and turn right on Notch Rd., which is a continuation N., along the range, of Rockwell Rd. You pass on the left open viewpoints westward to the Taconic Range. In 3.5 mi. from the fork, park on the right and walk another

100 yds. ahead to the AT crossing. Take this trail (white blazes) to the left, passing an open area called Tall Spruces over a rough section of trail. After .5 mi. of hiking, reach the Money Brook Trail going left from the AT. Before turning onto this trail, you may wish to continue on the AT another .5 mi. or so, ascending to an open section of the crest of Mt. Prospect where there is a fine view, northwest, of the Taconic Range and Williamstown. Retrace your steps down the AT and take the Money Brook Trail, now on your right, southwest, through a stand of red spruce trees. The trail is marked with triangular blue state forest markers. After about .3 mi. from the junction with the AT, turn right on a red-blazed side trail which takes you about 100 yds. to the Tall Spruces or Wilbur's Clearing. Back at the Money Brook Trail, you have a choice of routes, as described below.

You can turn left on this trail and retrace your route, turning right at the AT to reach Notch Rd. and your car. The other choice is to take a longer loop, involving some climbing, by going right farther along the Money Brook Trail. In about a third of a mi., turn left on a side trail with triangular blue painted blazes. As indicated by a sign, this goes to Notch Rd. on the east. There is a considerable climb up this trail to the road, where you turn left and walk down northward for a half-mile to your car.

APPENDICES

Hikes & Walks by Degree of Difficulty

Hikes and walks are ranked here by a simple system. Walks are rated "A," "B," or "C" — "A" being the easiest and "C" the most difficult. Hikes are rated "1," "2," or "3," with "1" being the easiest, "2" somewhat more challenging, and "3" the most difficult. Where specific distances and/or times are available, these, too, are cited for convenience.

Walk / Hike   **Difficulty / Distance / Time**

SOUTH COUNTY

Mount Washington
   Hikes: Alander Mountain/
        Bash Bish Falls 2   7 mi./3 hrs.
        Mount Everett.................. 2   5.5 mi./2.75 hrs.

Sheffield
   Walks: Salisbury Road .... A   7 mi./2.5 hrs.
        Bartholomew's Cobble/
        Ashley House .... B   approx. 2 hrs.

Egremont
   Walk: Baldwin Hill Road
        North & South .... A   6 mi./2.5 hrs.

New Marlborough
   Walks: Harmon Road .... A   7 mi./2.5 hrs.
        Campbell Falls .... A   4.5 mi./2 hrs.
        York Pond .... A   1 mi./30 min.

Great Barrington
   Walks: Seekonk .... A   3 or 6 mi./1 or 2 hrs.
        Benedict Pond .... A   5 mi./2 hrs.
   Hike: Monument Mountain 2   3 mi./1.5 hrs.

Tyringham
 Walk: Tyringham Cobble .... B 2 mi./ 1 hr.

Stockbridge
 Walks: Ice Glen .... C 3.5 mi./1.5 hrs.
    Bowker's Woods .... A 5 mi./15 min.
    Prospect Hill .... B 3 mi./1 hr.
    Glendale .... B various options
    Gould Meadows and
    Bullard Woods .... A various options

CENTRAL COUNTY

Lenox
 Walks: Kennedy Park .... A 3-4 mi./1.5 hrs.
    Reservoirs .... B 8 mi. or less
              3 hrs. or less
    Golden Hill .... B 2.5 mi./ 1hr.
 Hike: Pleasant Valley/
    Lenox Mountain .... 1 various options

Richmond
 Walk: East Road .... A 4.6 mi./ 2 hrs.

Peru
 Walk: Rice Sanctuary .... B various trails

Pittsfield
 Walks: Downtown .... A 8 blocks/30 min.
    Canoe Meadows .... A various trails
 Hike: Berry Pond .... 1 5 mi./ 2 hrs.

Hancock
 Hike: Shaker Mountain .... 2 6.5 mi./3 hrs.

Dalton
 Walk: Wahconah Falls .... A few hundred ft.

Windsor
 Walk: Windsor Jambs .... B 3 mi./1.5 hrs.
 Hike: Notchview/Judge's Hill ....1 5.5 mi./2.25 hrs.

NORTH COUNTY

Cheshire
    Walk: Hoosic River Railroad .... A   4.5 mi./2 hrs.

Adams and Mount Greylock
    Walks: Overlook Trail C   2.5 mi./1 hr.
             Campground Trails:
                Stony Ledge .... A   2 mi./50 min.
                March Cataract C   under 2 mi./45 min.
                Deer Hill C   2.25 mi./1 hr.
             Mount Prospect
             from Notch Road 2   1 mi./30 min.
    Hikes: Cheshire Harbor Trail 2   6.6 mi./2.5 hrs.
             Bellows Pipe Trail 3   4 mi./1.5 hrs.
             The Hopper 2   8 mi./3.5 hrs.
             Stony Ledge and
             Roaring Brook Trail 2   9 mi./3.75 hrs.

Williamstown
    Walk: Stone Hill .... B   1.5 mi./1 hr.
    Hikes: Berlin Mountain 3   5.25 mi./3 hrs.
             Pine Cobble and
             Broad Brook Trails 3   10 mi./5 hrs.
             RRR Brooks 3   7.75 mi./3 hrs.
             The Dome 2   6.4 mi./3 hrs.

North Adams
    Walk: The Cascades .... A   1 mi./30 min.

Florida and Savoy
    Walks: Borden Mountain and
             Tannery Falls .... B   various distances
    Hike: Spruce Hill 1   4 mi./1.5 hrs.

Florida and Monroe: Tunnel and Turbine
    Hike: Dunbar Brook 3   9 mi./4 hrs.

LONG HIKES AND
TRAIL SYSTEMS

Hikes & Walks in the Berkshire Hills is designed for day trippers, only tangentially describing the long-distance trails in the county. They are well covered in guides specific to them, noted here and in the bibliography. Nor does this book cover more than a fraction of the trails in the county. In particular, many more hikes in northern Berkshire are described in the Williams College Outing Club's guide.

The Appalachian Trail

In the 1920s, Benton McKaye and others used available state-owned land located between convenient small town inns and lodges to plan the Berkshire section of the 2,050-mi. footpath from Springer Mtn. in Georgia to Mt. Katahdin in Maine. It is intended to be a passive, recreational trail. No vehicles are allowed. The 262-mile Long Trail, the length of Vermont to the Canadian border, begins on the AT at the Vermont line, north of Pine Cobble.

The more than 86 miles of the AT in Berkshire enter in South County at Sage's Ravine and wander through Mt. Everett State Reservation, East Mtn. State Forest, Beartown State Forest, October Mtn. State Forest, Mt. Greylock State Reservation, and Clarksburg State Forest, in the north, from whence they exit the county. In recent years, the National Park Service has been attempting to move sections in between state forests onto protected lands and away from the original conception of connecting towns. The AT is blazed with white rectangles, with side trails blazed blue.

Shelters will eventually be placed within a day's hike of each other over the entire length of the trail. Bascom Lodge, on Mt. Greylock, is a storied rendezvous for through-hikers, who can get a reduced rate for a night in a real bed, cooked food, and showers by helping in the kitchen. See: *Appalachian Trail Guide — Massachusetts-Connecticut*.

The Mahican Mohawk Trail

The Appalachian Mtn. Club, Deerfield River Watershed Assoc., Friends of Mohawk Trail State Forest, and Hoosic River Watershed Assoc. are laying out a 100-mi. trail connecting the Connecticut and Hudson rivers by following the Deerfield and Hoosic rivers. Parts have been completed. The trail is marked by yellow disks with a green maple leaf.

Information is available at the starting point, Historic Deerfield (413-774-5881), or AMC (413-443-0011).

The Taconic Crest Trail

The Taconic Hiking Club, founded in 1932 in Troy, New York, sponsors various kinds of outings. In 1948 its members began to develop the Crest Trail, 29 miles from Berry Pond in Pittsfield State Forest to Prosser Hollow, New York. The trail runs generally north and south along a ridge through 3 states. The club also maintains 7 miles of the Taconic Skyline Trail from Berry Pond south to Rte. 20 in Pittsfield. The trail is marked by white diamond-shaped markers or paint; side trails are marked by blue diamonds. As well as Pittsfield State Forest, the TCT runs through newly acquired New York Department of Environmental Conservation property at Petersburgh Pass, Williams College's Hopkins Forest, and other private land. Once every other year, the club sponsors a 1-day, end-to-end hike, beginning with breakfast before dawn at Berry Pond and continuing past dusk. See: *Guide to the Taconic Crest Trail.*

The Taconic Trail System

The entire Taconic system includes the Taconic Crest Trail, the Taconic Skyline Trail, and the South Taconic Trail. The 23-mile-long Skyline Trail runs from Richmond to Williamstown, including the 7-mile section south of Berry Pond maintained by the Taconic Hiking Club. It follows along the Brodie Mtn. extension to the Taconics. About half is in Pittsfield State Forest and half on private land. The blazes are painted white, round or square in shape. The trail is not consistently maintained.

The South Taconic Trail extends 15.7 miles, mostly in New York State's Taconic State Park and Mt. Washington State Forest in Massachusetts. It runs parallel to the AT, to the west, and is maintained by volunteers from the New York chapter of the AMC, the Mid-Hudson chapter of the Adirondack Mountain Club, the New York/New Jersey Appalachian Trail Conference, and the Sierra Club. The crest it follows provides almost continuous, open, extensive views east and west, including Alander and Bash Bish (see the description of that hike). Numerous side trails and camping areas provide circuit routes. See: *Guide to the Taconic Trail System.*

Williams Outing Club Trails

Founded by Albert Hopkins as the Alpine Club in 1863, the Williams Outing Club is the oldest mountain-climbing organization in the United States, preceding both the White Mtn. and Appalachian Mtn. clubs. Volunteer college students maintain some 75 miles of trails in northern Berkshire, southern Vermont, and eastern New York. Its trail guide (see Williams Outing Club's *Trail Map and Guide*) details trips on 35 trails in the Williamstown area.

BOOTS, BOOKS, MAPS, PACKS

Stores throughout the county sell items useful to hikers, for example, ice cream cones. Nevertheless, certain kinds of stores are of particular value.

SPORTING GOODS

South County

Appalachian Mountain Gear, 413-528-8811; 684 S. Main St., Great Barrington.

Gerry Cosby & Co., 413-229-6600; 103 S. Under Mountain Rd., Sheffield.

Rick Moon's Outdoors, 413-528-4666; 107 Stockbridge Rd., Great Barrington.

Central County

Arcadian Shop, 413-637-3010; 91 Pittsfield-Lenox Rd. (Rte. 7), Lenox.

Champ Sports, 413-448-2123; Berkshire Mall, Lanesborough.

Dave's Sporting Goods, 413-442-2960; 1164 North St., Pittsfield.

Dick Moon Sporting Goods, 413-442-8281; 114 Fenn St., Pittsfield.

Marshall Sporting Goods, Inc., 413-443-4595; 207 Elm St., Pittsfield.

Main Street Sports and Leisure, 413-637-4407, 800-952-9197; 48 Main St., Lenox.

North County

Berkshire Outfitters, 413-743-5900; Route 8, Adams.

Goff's Sports, 413-458-3605; 15 Spring St., Williamstown.

The Mountain Goat, 413-458-8445; 130 Water St., Williamstown.

Points North Outfitters, 413-743-4030; Rte. 8, on Adams/Cheshire line.

The Sports Corner, 413-664-8654; 61 Main St., North Adams.

BOOKSTORES

South County

Apple Tree Books, 413-243-2012; 87 Main St, Lee.

The Bookloft, 413-528-1521; Barrington Plaza, Stockbridge Rd., Rte. 7, Gt. Barrington.

Yellow House Books, 413-528-8227; 252 Main St., Gt. Barrington.

Central County

Barnes & Noble, 413-496-9051; Berkshire Crossing Mall, Rte. 9, Pittsfield.

Berkshire Book Shop, 413-442-0165; 164 North St., Pittsfield.
The Bookstore, 413-637-3390; 9 Housatonic St., Lenox.
Stockbridge News, 413-298-0109; 6 Elm St., Stockbridge.
Waldenbooks, 413-499-0115; Berkshire Mall, Lanesborough.

North County
Crystal Unicorn Bookstore, 413-664-7377; 59 Main St., No. Adams
Papyri Books, 413-662-2099; 49 Main St., No. Adams
Water Street Books, 413-458-8071; 26 Water St., Williamstown.

BIBLIOGRAPHY

Appalachian Trail Guide to Massachusetts-Connecticut (1988),
P.O. 807, Harpers Ferry, WV, 25425-0807.
Binzen, William. *The Berkshires* (a book of photographs)
(1986), Globe Pequot Press, Chester CT.
Brady and White. *Fifty Hikes in Massachusetts* (1983),
Backcountry Publications, P.O. 175, Woodstock, VT 05091.
Burns and Stevens. *Most Excellent Majesty: A History of Mount
Greylock* (1988), Berkshire House Publishers, 480 Pleasant St.,
Suite 5, Lee, MA 01238.
Cuyler, Lewis. *Bike Rides in the Berkshire Hills* (1990), Berkshire
House Publishers, 480 Pleasant St., Suite 5, Lee, MA 01238.
Drew, Bernard. *A History of Notchview* (1986), Attic Revivals Press,
Gt. Barrington, MA 01230.
Federal Writers Project. *The Berkshire Hills* (1939), reprinted by
Northeastern Univ. Press (1987).
Griswold, Whit. *Berkshire Trails for Walking and Ski Touring* (1986),
The East Woods Press (out-of-print).
Ryan, Christopher J. *Guide to the Taconic Trail System* (1989), New
England Cartographics, P.O. Box 369, Amherst, MA 01004.
Sternfield, Jonathan, and Lauren R. Stevens. *The Berkshire Book: A
Complete Guide* (4th ed., 1997), Berkshire House Publishers, 480
Pleasant St., Suite 5, Lee, MA 01238.
Taconic Hiking Club. *Guide to the Taconic Crest Trail* (1988), 810
Church St., Troy, NY 12180.
Thoreau, Henry David. *A Week on the Concord and Merrimack
Rivers* (1893), Houghton Mifflin Co., Boston, MA.
Williams Outing Club. *Trail Guide and Map* (1989), Williams
College, Williamstown, MA 01267.

A Note on the Author

Lauren R. Stevens has lived and walked in Berkshire County for 30 years. He is the author with Deborah Burns of *Most Excellent Majesty: A History of Mount Greylock*, of *Skiing in the Berkshire Hills*, and (with Richard Babcock) of *Old Barns in the New World*. In 1982 he founded *The Advocate*, a weekly newspaper, and he continues to write for that publication. He has also written on outdoor recreation and the environment for most Berkshire regional publications, and he has published a novel, *The Double Axe* (Scribners). He is Executive Director of the Hoosic River Watershed Association. The father of three, Lauren Stevens lives in Williamstown, where he has taught and served as Dean of Freshmen for Williams College.